Knowing God
by Name

Knowing God
by Name

Names of God That Bring Hope and Healing

David Wilkerson

Chosen Books

A Division of Baker Book House Co
Grand Rapids, Michigan 49516

© 2001, 2003 by David Wilkerson Publications, Inc.

Published by Chosen Books
a division of Baker Publishing Group
P.O. Box 6287, Grand Rapids, MI 49516-6287
www.chosenbooks.com

Previously published in 2001 under the title *Hallowed Be Thy Names* by David Wilkerson Publications, Inc.

Seventh printing, May 2006

Printed in the United States of America

Library of Congress Cataloging-in-Publication Data
Wilkerson, David R.
    Knowing God by name : names of God that bring hope and healing / David Wilkerson.
        p.   cm.
    ISBN 10: 0-8007-9342-0 (pbk.)
    ISBN 978-0-8007-9342-5 (pbk.)
    1. God—Name. I. Title.
BT180.N2W53 2003
231—dc21   2003009313

Scripture is taken from the King James Version of the Bible.

Contents

Introduction

Many books have been written about the names of God. Most of these are scholarly works, exploring the deepest theological meanings behind each of God's names. They are exhaustive, covering the 23 compound names of God found in Scripture, as well as the more than forty compound names of Jehovah.

In writing this book I have chosen not to cover every name of God. Nor have I sought to study every theological nuance of the names I cover. My purpose in exploring this subject has been to obtain a heart-knowledge of God's names. I wanted to have a personal revelation of His names—to appropriate their fullest meaning for my daily walk with Him.

You see, each of God's names reveals a defining quality of His nature and character. As I searched the Scriptures, I discovered that God revealed these names to His people only as they needed them—in their moments of deepest crisis. It dawned on me that this is how I want to learn my Lord's nature also: to understand His heart toward us in our most desperate times. That is why I have chosen to explore the names of God that relate to my own times of testing and crisis.

Simply put, this book is for weary or hurting believers who need assurance and hope in their times of trial. In my opinion, that includes every devoted servant of Jesus Christ! Scripture makes it abundantly clear that, because of our commitment to the Lord, we are going to be put through the fire of testing. That is the very reason God revealed His names to His people in the first place: to bring them encouragement, hope and life.

Why is it important for us to know these names of God? Here are just two of the reasons the Bible gives us.

First, various psalms tell us that we receive God's deliverance through knowing His name. "Our help is in the name of the LORD, who made heaven and earth" (Psalm 124:8). "Because he has known my name . . . I will deliver him" (Psalm 91:15). "I found trouble and sorrow. Then called I upon the name of the LORD. . . . I was brought low, and he helped me" (Psalm 116:3–4, 6).

Second, Isaiah writes that God keeps us close when we trust in His name. "Who is among you that feareth the LORD, that obeyeth the voice of his servant, that walketh in darkness, and hath no light? Let him trust in the name of the LORD, and stay upon his God" (Isaiah 50:10).

In reality, God refers to Himself by only one name. In the Bible, He calls Himself the great I AM. "God said unto Moses, I AM THAT I AM: and he said, Thus shalt thou say unto the children of Israel, I AM hath sent me unto you" (Exodus 3:14).

What does the Lord mean by saying His name is I AM? He is telling us that He is the everlasting one—the true God, with no beginning and no end. He always was, He is right now and He always will be. As He explained to Moses, "I AM whatever you need, at any point in your life. That is My nature—to be for you whatever you need at any given time. My name is I AM—and I want My people to remember it."

Although "I AM" is the only name God gave for Himself, the ancient Hebrews also referred to Him by several other names in order to help describe His nature and character. These names are expressions of who our Lord is and what He is like.

It is important to note that we can know someone's name without having any clear idea of who that person is or what he is like. This is true with God also. We can memorize all of the Lord's various names, and yet still have only the vaguest idea of who He truly is. I believe this is why He revealed His names to the Israelites during their trials and crises. He wanted them to learn every facet of His loving nature toward them, and He used difficult situations as the best way to impress truth on their hearts.

Is this not how our children get to know us? If someone were to ask my children, "Who is your father and what is he like?", I would be grieved if all they could give were the basics: "His name is David Wilkerson. He lives in New York City and pastors a church in Times Square. During my childhood, he put a roof over my head and always put food on the table. He took care of me well."

This says nothing about my relationship with my children. Even if they were to add, "He's also a good father," it would not capture what I hope I am in my relationship to them. I hope that I have been a good father to them over the years—rejoicing over them in love, being patient with their failures, available to them at all times, offering counsel and meeting their needs. Like any loving dad, I want my relationship with my children to go beyond fulfilling my duties. In fact, I want them to know me *mostly* by my caring heart toward them.

At times we are asked by nonbelievers, "You say you know God. Tell me, who is He and what's He like?" All some Christians can answer is, "He's the great I AM. He rules over heaven and earth and He sits on His throne in glory." They have nothing to say about our heavenly Father's loving relationship with us.

When my children were growing up, I never had to lecture them about what I am like. I never had to say, "I'm your father—I'm patient, kind, full of mercy and loving kindness toward you. I'm tenderhearted over you, ready to forgive you at all times." They would have laughed if I had stood up at the dinner table and made a proclamation like that. Why? My kids learned about my love for them during their crisis experiences. They saw my love toward them when they were embarrassed, hurt by life or in need of forgiveness. Now, as they are grown and married with children of their own, my sons and daughters are getting to know me through a whole new set of experiences. They are learning even more about me by my attitudes and actions toward them in this new time of need in their lives.

So it is with us in getting to know our heavenly Father. From the time of Adam down through the cross of Christ, the Lord gave His people ever-increasing revelations of His character. He did not do this simply by proclaiming who He is. He did not try to reveal Himself by announcing to Abraham or Moses: "The following names describe My nature: *El Elyon, El Shaddai, Jehovah Jireh, Jehovah Rophi, Jehovah Makkeh, Jehovah Nissi, Jehovah Tsebaioth, Jehovah Shalom, Jehovah Tsidkenu, Jehovah Shammah,* etc. Now go and learn these, and you will discover who I am."

These Hebrew expressions do describe the wondrous glories and provisions that are wrapped up in our Lord's character, but God revealed these aspects of His nature by actually doing for His people what He proclaimed Himself to be. Time and again He saw His children's need, foresaw the enemy's strategy against them and intervened supernaturally on their behalf.

As you read this book I urge you to get to know your heavenly Father slowly and purposefully, on a heart-to-heart level. You do not need to memorize all of these hallowed names in their Hebrew forms. For example, do not memorize God's name *Jehovah Tse-*

baioth—simply learn that He is the Lord of Hosts. Get to know the English meanings of His names and remember them.

I suggest that you read only one chapter at a sitting. You could keep this book on your nightstand, for instance, and try a chapter each night. Then, when you have finished, go back over the chapters that ministered to you while you were in difficulty. As you review those chapters ask the Holy Ghost to remind you of the many ways God has been there for you during your times of need. Ask the Spirit to build in you a true heart-knowledge of I AM—the God who is everything you need.

Pronunciation of the Names of God in This Book

El Elyon	El Ely-OWN
El Shaddai	El Shad-DI
Jehovah Jireh	Je-HO-va JI-rah
Jehovah Rophi	Je-HO-va RO-fee
Jehovah Makkeh	Je-HO-va MA-keh
Jehovah Nissi	Je-HO-va NEE-see
Jehovah Tsebaioth	Je-HO-va Se-baw-OT
Jehovah Shalom	Je-HO-va Shaw-LOME
Jehovah Tsidkenu	Je-HO-va Sid-KAY-noo
Jehovah Shammah	Je-HO-va SHAW-mah
Jehovah Rohi	Je-HO-va RO-ee

one

El Elyon • El Shaddai • Jehovah Jireh

God Most High, Creator and Possessor of Heaven and Earth
God All-Powerful and All-Sufficient
The Lord Who Sees and Who Provides

The fourteenth chapter of Genesis describes the first war ever recorded in human history. A confederation of kings declared war on the cities of Sodom and Gomorrah, and the two sides waged a battle in the "vale of Siddim." The attackers won and "the kings of Sodom and Gomorrah fled, and fell there; and they that remained fled to the mountain" (Genesis 14:10).

The invading forces then pillaged Sodom and Gomorrah, capturing the people and securing all their wealth, food and supplies. "They took all the goods of Sodom and Gomorrah, and all their victuals, and went their way" (verse 11). During this invasion, "They took Lot, Abram's brother's son, who dwelt in Sodom" (verse 12).

Now, the Bible tells us that Abram had 318 "trained servants" (verse 14). This phrase indicates that these men were practiced in the art of war. Evidently the servants were trained to protect the interests of Abram's clan from plunder. Abram was determined to recover Lot and his family, so he led his servants in hot pursuit of the confederated army. When Abram and his militia had traveled some 140 miles, they finally overtook the invaders. They defeated the enemy soundly—a rout so lopsided that the fleeing soldiers left behind all the spoils they had stolen. Abram ended up rescuing all of the captives, including Lot, and recovering all of Sodom and Gomorrah's goods.

As we pick up the story in verse seventeen, Abram and his men are heading back over a ridge in the valley just north of Salem. What a sight Abram's caravan must have been! It was led by a bold man of God and followed by his troop of servant-soldiers, Lot and his family, the freed citizens of Sodom and Gomorrah, and all the treasures and food supplies taken by the confederation of kings.

As I picture this scene I cannot help wondering: Why did God allow Abram to save Sodom and Gomorrah? After all, God knew that they soon were to be judged. Why not tell Abram to rescue only Lot and his family, and let the wicked Sodomites be taken captive?

My personal belief is that God used Abram to prevent Satan from preempting His divine judgment. No doubt the devil knew that God planned to destroy Sodom. Satan may have hoped that, as prisoners in other countries, the citizens of Sodom and Gomorrah would spread their perverted lifestyle to other heathen nations. The devil would have had an army of "missionaries" spreading moral decay throughout the then-known world!

But God stopped Satan in his tracks. He used Abram to bring back all the people of Sodom and Gomorrah to face His divine judgment. By doing so, God was quarantining them. Now He could burn out the disease from their vile society and stop it from spreading.

Abram Encounters Two Kings

Upon his victorious return from the battle, Abram was met by two kings—the king of Salem and the king of Sodom. These kings offer fascinating contrasts.

First, as Abram approached the city of Salem, which means "peaceful" and is generally identified as the ancient city of Jerusalem, the king came out to meet him. This king was named Melchizedek, and the Bible refers to this mysterious figure in only three verses. The first, Genesis 14:18, describes him as both "king of Salem" and "priest of the most high God." This dual description of king and priest alerts us to Melchizedek's role as a type—a living picture—of Christ Himself. Indeed, Melchizedek's meeting with Abram was an amazing visitation. First, acting as priest, Melchizedek served Abram a covenant meal of bread and wine. Then, acting as king, Melchizedek accepted a tithe from Abram. Afterward Melchizedek disappeared from the picture as suddenly as he had appeared. This man clearly foreshadows the Person and work of Jesus Christ.

The second reference in Scripture to the King of Salem was written one thousand years after his meeting with Abram. Speaking prophetically of the Messiah, King David states: "Thou art a priest for ever after the order of Melchizedek" (Psalm 110:4). Then, one thousand years after that, the writer of Hebrews confirms that this ancient king's continual priesthood (see Hebrews 7:3) does indeed represent Jesus' eternal priesthood: "Thou [Jesus] art a priest for ever after the order of Melchisedec" (Hebrews 7:17).

Soon after his incredible meeting with Melchizedek, Abram was addressed by the king of Sodom. This king had fled the battlefield as the confederation of armies prevailed. Then he had had to sit by and watch as Abram carried the day. Now, as the king saw Abram returning in victory, he offered to him all the spoils of battle. The king told Abram, "Give me the persons, and take the goods to thyself" (Genesis 14:21).

To gain the full impact of the king's offer here, we need to examine the scene more closely. Here was godly Abram, leading home all the freed captives of Sodom and Gomorrah. Satan must have been enraged at the sight. His plan, I suspect, for spreading Sodom's wickedness had been demolished. He was probably seething! I can imagine his thoughts running along these lines: "This holy man has become the people's hero and deliverer. Worse, I just saw him communing with Melchizedek, the priest of God! The Lord must be planning to convert all of these Sodomites."

At that point, I believe, the devil filled Sodom's king with a spirit of jealousy. You can almost hear Satan's scheming voice speaking through this vile king: "Keep all the spoils, Abram. You can have everything we possess. Just give me back my people." In reality, the devil was pleading, "Please, Abram—take everything you want. Just don't take these souls away from me."

You must understand: The goods that Sodom's king offered to Abram were more than just a wagonload of groceries. These were the spoils of two prosperous city-states: thousands of cattle, sheep, camels, donkeys, weapons, clothing and furnishings—treasures of gold, silver, diamonds, jewels and precious stones.

Yet Abram refused the offer without hesitation. He told the king, "I have lift up mine hand unto the LORD, the most high God, the possessor of heaven and earth, that I will not take from a thread even to a shoelatchet, and that I will not take any thing that is thine, lest thou shouldest say, I have made Abram rich" (Genesis 14:22–23). Abram was saying, in essence, "You can have the people and all the riches. *I'm taking Lot and his family with me.*"

Facing These Two Kings in Our Own Lives

When we believers give our hearts to Jesus, we win a great battle. We defeat the powers of hell, robbing Satan of the spoils he took from us when he ruled our lives. But afterward, as we are still glowing with spiritual victory and freedom, just down the road, two "kings" await us—symbolized by the same two kings who awaited Abram.

Abram faced as strong a temptation as any human being has ever experienced. Before him was an offer of riches, material goods and fame. It would not have compromised Abram's reputation to accept it, but he did not even think twice about his decision. His response to the king's offer was a quick and clear no. Why? Because what mattered most to Abram was preserving *God's* reputation. In effect he was telling the king of Sodom, "I'm returning all of these things to you—the people, the riches, everything. My Lord owns them all anyway. If He decides to make me wealthy, so be it. But I don't want you to be able to brag that you made me rich."

Where did Abram get such detachment from this world and the independence to reject outright the devil's offer? How did he obtain this tremendous authority to be able to refuse such a powerful temptation?

Abram derived his strength from a fresh revelation of who God is. You see, Melchizedek had opened Abram's eyes to an amazing vision of God's character: "He [Melchizedek] blessed him, and said, Blessed be Abram of the most high God, possessor of heaven and earth: and blessed be the most high God, which hath delivered thine enemies into thy hand" (Genesis 14:19–20).

Embedded in this verse is a name for Jehovah God: *El Elyon.* It means, literally, "God Most High, creator and possessor of heaven and earth." Melchizedek was declaring to Abram, "Your Lord is not just the greatest of all the gods. He is the creator of the entire universe. Everything in it belongs to Him—all wealth, cattle, possessions. He is in control of everything you see around you."

This name, *El Elyon,* provided Abram with a new discovery about the Lord. He had known God as the Lord who called him out of the land of Ur, but not as Lord Most High, creator and possessor of all things. Now Abram was convinced that God had everything under control.

Abram rejoiced over this marvelous discovery as he left his meeting with Melchizedek. That is why the patriarch spoke to the king of Sodom with an oath: "I have sworn to the Lord God Most High," he said (see verse 22). It was as though he was saying, "From now on, I am going to trust only *El Elyon* to meet all my needs. If the Lord creates and possesses all things, then I won't accept a single shoelace from this Sodomite society. I don't want to depend on any man. Instead, I am going to put my life, my family and my future totally into God's care."

With this new understanding of who God was, Abram had the power and faith to face any temptation. Abram saw Sodom's goods as trivial. He scoffed at the king's offer: "You offer me trinkets, Sodom, when my God owns the universe. He possesses the spoils of the whole earth. The Lord alone is my supply, all I will ever need. So take your stuff and go. *El Elyon* has made me an offer I cannot refuse."

Abram's faith must have been totally rejuvenated at this point. I imagine him reasoning, "Lord, if You possess all that exists in heaven and earth, then possess me, too. I want You to take control of my life; rule over everything I am and everything I do!" Of course, Abram did eventually become God-possessed, and at that point his faith began to soar, increasing with every thought of the wondrous revelation God had given him.

Every devoted Christian has discovered the Lord as his Savior from sin. Yet have we also discovered Him as *El Elyon*—God Most High, creator and possessor of all things? Have we begun to see Him with new eyes as Abram did? Are we convinced that He holds our entire lives and well-being in His hands?

Hebrews tells us that our Lord never changes—that He is the same yesterday, today and forever (see Hebrews 13:8). Are you persuaded that God is in absolute control over all things in your own life? Are you able to face the storms, tests and trials in your life, calmly testifying, "My God, *El Elyon,* has everything under control"? Do you trust His power to help you resist every temptation the devil throws at you? Can you trust that if God has created a new heart in you, He also has the power to create in you a hunger and thirst to know Him more intimately?

We obtain this kind of power only by laying hold of the revelation that our God is *El Elyon.* In contemporary terms, this revelation means, "God is boss of everything. That means there are no accidents in my life—no such things as fate, happenstance or luck, either good or bad. Every step I take is ordered by the Lord. Everything in my life—in fact, everything in this universe—is under His control. His Word tells me that Satan cannot tempt me any more than I can bear. My boss is always faithful to show me the way of escape."

Abram's Revelation Brings a Challenge

Armed with his new discovery about God, Abram took the opportunity to challenge the Lord about a promise made years earlier: "Abram said, Behold, to me thou hast given no seed: and, lo, one born in my house is mine heir" (Genesis 15:3). It is as if Abram were saying, "Lord, I know You are *El Elyon,* creator and possessor of all things. So where is my promised child?

You said I would be the father of many nations. Yet here I am, still childless after all these years." God wanted Abram to hold fast to his faith. He responded by entering into covenant with Abram, making an oath to him that sealed His promise of a son (see verse 18).

For some reason, though, Abram's faith did begin to waver. You know the story: After so many years of trying, Abram's wife, Sarai, seemed unable to bear children. So she offered her hand-maid, Hagar, to Abram to sire a son. At that point Abram took matters into his own hands. He impregnated the handmaid, who bore a son, Ishmael.

Abram was 86 years old when Ishmael was born. He hoped the boy would provide the seed God had promised. But in the Lord's eyes, this child was illegitimate because he was not the child of faith and promise.

More years passed and there was no sign that Sarai would ever bear a child. Abram and Sarai just kept getting older. By the time Ishmael turned 13, Abram was 99 years old. He must have been on the verge of losing all hope that God's promise would ever be fulfilled. Once again, his faith was being tried.

I believe Scripture is making a point here for everyone who has chosen to follow Jesus. It is saying that God uses our crises—the most difficult, trying times in our lives— to give us hopeful revelations of who He is. Each revelation is like a separate ray of light reflecting from a diamond: It reveals a different aspect of our Lord's nature, giving us fresh views of His character and power toward us. These revelations shine especially brightly during our times of darkness. Those are the most effective times for Him to reveal to us His ability and desire to deliver us.

As Abram faced this ongoing personal crisis, the Lord decided once again to give His servant a fresh revelation of Himself. He wanted Abram to be fully persuaded of His faithfulness. Scripture says, "When Abram was ninety years old and nine, the LORD appeared to Abram, and said unto him, I am the Almighty God; walk before me, and be thou perfect" (Genesis 17:1).

The Hebrew phrase for "Almighty God" here is *El Shaddai*. The literal meaning of this name is "God, all-powerful and all-sufficient." What an incredible revelation for Abram to receive at this time! God was speaking very personally to His servant here, saying, "Abram, you already know I have power over every condition in your life. I have convinced you that I am in control of all things—that there are no accidents in your life, no situations that are merely fate or luck. I am the head, the chief, the boss of all creation, and My word is eternal. Now I am going to tell you something else about My nature that you need to understand to continue in faith.

"I am not only in control of all things, but I always keep My word. No obstacle can keep My word from coming to pass. I am not bound by the laws of nature or fettered by any man. I can do anything at any time. There are no mountains too high for Me, no valleys too low, no rivers or oceans too wide. When I say something is going to be done, it is already done. Nothing can stop My promise. I am *El Shaddai*—all-powerful, all-sufficient keeper of My promises. I guarantee My word."

God saw that Abram was focusing on all the impossibilities of his situation. Abram simply could not see past his age, his dried-up body and Sarai's dead womb. So the Lord revealed Himself to Abram specifically as the God who gives life to the dead. He opened Abram's eyes to the part of His nature that performs the impossible.

Once Abram received this revelation, he believed God was who He claimed to be. Abram "was strong in faith, giving glory to God; and being fully persuaded that, what he had promised, he was able also to perform" (Romans 4:20–21). This godly man knew that God could not lie. The Lord had sworn to make him a father of all nations; surely God would do what He said He would do.

Abram's newfound faith eventually brought forth the child Isaac, the promised heir. It also brought Abram his new name, *Abraham,* "father of a multitude." Now Abraham and his Lord were united in a special realm of faith. Moreover, Abraham had discovered the secret to walking uprightly before God.

Discovering the Secret That Abraham Knew

Here is the secret to a godly walk: We are to *receive*—to acknowledge, believe, embrace and act upon—the revelation God gives us of who He is. That is the secret, plain and simple. We are able to walk uprightly before the Lord, but not because we have willpower, knowledge or even a covenant promise in hand. We walk uprightly because we are fully persuaded that *El Shaddai* will keep His promises to us.

The evidence of such faith is a restful heart. If your soul is not at rest, you are not really living in faith. Conversely, if you believe God is who He says He is, and that He is faithful to do what He has promised to do, then you do not have a worry in the world. Faith is being confident that all things work together for good to those who love the Lord and are called according to His purpose (see Romans 8:28). God has already promised that He will not let the devil have you; nor will He allow anything to happen to you beyond what is common to every other human being (see 1 Corinthians 10:13). In the midst of every temptation, the Lord promises to make a way of escape for you so you will be able to bear up under the pressure (see 1 Corinthians 10:13).

God had given Abraham the following covenant promise: "I am thy shield, and thy exceeding great reward" (Genesis 15:1). This is known as the Abrahamic covenant. The Lord vowed to Abraham, "None of your enemies can harm you. I will always be faithful to deliver you, no matter what your circumstances. I will personally be your reward. You are eternally Mine, Abraham. I am going to maintain you, protect you and keep you for Myself."

Why were these promises so important to Abraham? Let me remind you, this man lived in a brutal and wicked society. His neighbors, in the region of the lower Jordan, led wild, dissolute lives. God had declared that their "cup of iniquity" was filling up and they would come under judgment. The Lord's assuring words enabled Abraham to lead a holy life in the midst of such abounding iniquity. How? Abraham believed what God said: that he was safe from all harm because the Lord was all-sufficient to keep His servant victorious over every evil.

The same is true for us today. I am convinced that only by embracing the revelation of God's covenant names will we be able to lead godly lives. Have you discovered your *El Shaddai,* all-sufficient God? It is time for you to stop focusing on your own weaknesses, powerlessness and failures.

Instead, believe God's promises to you. He has pledged to keep you, teach you, put His fear in you, cause you to walk in His ways, give you His Holy Spirit and blot out all your sins and replace them with His loving kindness. Will you rest in the promise that He will be all-sufficient for you?

Abraham's Supreme Test of Obedience and Faith

Abraham enjoyed a season of peace and quiet with his son of faith, Isaac. The boy's name means "laughter" and, indeed, this miracle child was the joy of Abraham's old age. Yet when Isaac was a young man, the Lord called upon Abraham for a supreme act of obedience. God told Abraham, "Take now thy son, thine only son Isaac, whom thou lovest, and get thee into the land of Moriah; and offer him there for a burnt offering upon one of the mountains which I will tell thee of" (Genesis 22:2).

When Abraham heard this word, he immediately began splitting wood for the trip. Then he gathered Isaac, two servants and a donkey and set out for Mount Moriah. The mountain was some fifty or sixty miles away and it would have taken the group about three days to get there. You can be sure that Abraham had plenty of time to think along the way. This had to have been the most trying, anguished time of his life! In his mind, his son was already dead. Abraham himself was now nearly 130 years old, and Isaac was about 30. The patriarch had watched his son grow into manhood—laughing with him, hugging him and teaching him the ways of the Lord. Now, after years of childlessness and waiting for God's promise to be fulfilled, he was being asked to give up the one thing dearest to his heart.

God's instruction to Abraham had to be as confusing as it was anguishing. Abraham knew Isaac was the promised seed through whom nations would come. This was the son he and Sarah had waited to have for so long, the one who would provide the very lineage of the Messiah. (We know Abraham was aware of this, because John 8:56 records Jesus as saying: "Your father Abraham rejoiced to see my day; and he saw it, and was glad.")

Nevertheless Abraham gave up his son in full faith. Think about it: He made the journey without once questioning God on the matter. Can you imagine the strength this required? We have to remember, Abraham was a human being just like us, with similar feelings and weaknesses. Yet he made a difficult decision to obey the Lord, based only on faith. Where did Abraham get the faith to obey such a hard word?

It came directly from the revelation of God's name. Abraham reminded himself, "My Lord has told me He is the creator of all things, and I believe Him. So, even if I slay my son, I know God has the power to raise him up. I am convinced of His resurrection power." Hebrews confirms Abraham's belief, telling us, "By faith Abraham, when he was tried, offered up Isaac: and he that had received the promises offered up his only begotten son . . . accounting that God was able to raise him up, even from the dead" (Hebrews 11:17–19).

When Abraham arrived at the foot of Mount Moriah, he instructed his two servants to stay behind while he and Isaac went to make sacrifice. Even at this point, Abraham demonstrated great faith. He told his servants, "I and the lad will go yonder and worship, and come again to you" (Genesis 22:5). He was telling them, "You'll see us both go up the mountain—and you'll see us both return."

Abraham made his way up the mountain, carrying the sacrificial knife and the burning censer. Isaac walked behind him carrying the wood and, at one point, spoke up: "Isaac spake unto Abraham his father, and said, My father: and he said, Here am I, my son. And he said, Behold the fire and the wood: but where is the lamb for a burnt offering? And Abraham said, My son, God will provide himself a lamb for a burnt offering: so they went both of them together" (verses 7–8).

In many ways this scene foreshadows the event of the cross. Isaac, the sacrificial son, carried wood up a hill, just as God's own Son, Jesus, would do. And Abraham willingly offered up his son as a sacrifice for sin, just as the heavenly Father would do. Moreover, during the three days' journey Abraham considered his son as already being dead. Yet when it was finished, Isaac emerged from the trip as if he had been raised from the dead. This prefigures the three days Jesus was dead before God raised Him up.

You may wonder, "Why would the Lord demand a human sacrifice, when the Old Testament tells us He hated that practice?" God was birthing a church, a nation of faith, through this event. This whole scenario was crucial in showing later generations that animal sacrifice could not atone for human sin. One day, there would have to be a human sacrifice, one that was holy and pure, and it would involve someone willing to lay down His life for all of humankind. Simply put, Abraham's journey was an illustrated sermon about the Messiah. It pointed to the future sacrifice made by Jesus Christ for the sins of the world.

Our focus in this passage, however, is a new discovery that God gave to Abraham. What was this discovery? It was another great revelation of His name.

When they finally arrived at the mountaintop, Abraham prepared to slay his son. As he bound Isaac and laid him upon the altar, the son must have obliged. After all, Isaac was an adult and his elderly father could never have wrestled him down. For this reason I believe that Isaac acted in faith as well. His father had taught him the covenant as he grew up, and Isaac had also learned the revelation of God's names. Thus, Isaac must have believed in the Lord's all-sufficiency as well. Like his father, he knew that even if he died, God had the power to raise him up again. Whether or not God chose to resurrect him, he would lay down his life in obedience to the Lord's command to Abraham. (This attitude also prefigured Christ, who willingly offered himself as the lamb to be sacrificed.)

What is the point of this scene for Christians who read it today? It is this: Almost all new discoveries of God—all fresh revelations of His Person, nature and character—are tied to some crisis, some intense human experience.

I stated earlier that we often discover more of our loving Father's nature during our difficult times. It was during Sodom's crisis that God revealed Himself to Abraham as *El Elyon*—God Most High, creator and possessor of all things. Likewise, it was during Abraham's own crisis of doubt that God revealed His name as *El Shaddai*—God all-powerful and all-sufficient. Now God was leading Abraham into the greatest crisis any human being could ever experience—the sacrifice of his own child. Yet, out of this crisis Abraham would receive the greatest revelation he could ever know about the heavenly Father.

As the time neared for Abraham to raise the knife, he was already walking in mature faith. He could face this test of obedience now, because he trusted in the revelations God had given him. In each case, he had received God's Word and mixed it with faith, taking its truth to heart. By this time he had appropriated the power of each of God's names in his life. And now, as Abraham stood over his son, he was ready to obey God perfectly. He remembered the Lord's

Knowing God by Name

revelation of Himself as *El Elyon,* creator of all things. Therefore, it would be a small matter for God to raise up Isaac from the dead. In addition, Abraham believed in *El Shaddai*—God all-sufficient, the one who keeps His word. The Lord had already assured him, "I have given you a son, Abraham, and you are going to see entire nations come out of him." It is clear that Abraham was acting on a faith founded solely on God's revealed promises.

Now this godly man lifted the knife. He was ready to thrust it through the heart of his beloved son. Then, suddenly, he was stopped by a voice from heaven:

> And the angel of the LORD called unto him out of heaven, and said, Abraham, Abraham: and he said, Here am I. And he said, Lay not thine hand upon the lad, neither do thou any thing unto him: for now I know that thou fearest God, seeing thou hast not withheld thy son, thine only son from me. And Abraham lifted up his eyes, and looked, and behold behind him a ram caught in a thicket by his horns: and Abraham went and took the ram, and offered him up for a burnt offering in the stead of his son. And Abraham called the name of that place Jehovah-jireh.
>
> Genesis 22:11–14

What an amazing miracle of provision! The whole time that Abraham was preparing to slay his son, God had a sacrificial animal ready nearby. The Lord must have supernaturally given that ram an appetite, causing it to wander up the hillside. As the animal foraged for food, its horns got tangled in a bush.

Here was a glorious new discovery of God's nature. He revealed Himself to Abraham as *Jehovah Jireh,* "the Lord who sees." In contemporary terms, this phrase translates as, "God will see to it." It is a name that speaks of provision.

We see this meaning illustrated in a later verse in the same chapter: "And Bethuel begat Rebekah" (Genesis 22:23). Let me explain the connection here. At the very moment Abraham was raising the knife over Isaac, his nephew Bethuel was raising the girl whom God would eventually give to Isaac as a wife. It is as if the Holy Spirit were telling Abraham, "Yes, I have kept My promise by saving your son. I have also provided for your heir; your brother's wife has already given birth to the girl Isaac will marry."

Isaac would not meet Rebekah for another several years down the road. But this passage proves the nature of *Jehovah Jireh,* the provider: Even before we call out to Him, our God answers. Long before we are even born, He is at work forming and shaping the circumstances of our lives.

The name *Jehovah Jireh* also has another meaning: "God is showing us." In other words, our Lord will reveal to us everything we need to obey Him. He will see to it that we are provided with all the power, strength and resolve to do whatever He commands.

I have seen men point to their new cars and, smiling, say, "Jehovah Jireh." In short, they are declaring, "See what God provided for me." But if you see *Jehovah Jireh* only as a supplier of material things, you do not have the true revelation of this glorious name! Our God is all of that, but He is much more besides. The apostle Paul describes the full meaning of this name when he writes, "My God shall supply all your need according to his riches in glory *by Christ Jesus*" (Philippians 4:19, emphasis added).

Our Lord promised to wipe away all our sins—and He did it. *Jehovah Jireh* saw to it that the penalties for our sins would be paid through His Son, Jesus Christ. Today our Lord promises that the Holy Spirit will provide us with the power we need to obey His word. He has written these words above His every command: "Your God will see to it that you obey Him. *Jehovah Jireh* will keep His promise to provide all faith and strength for you, through the power of the Holy Spirit."

But What If Abraham Had Failed?

You may wonder, "Even though God provided Abraham with the ram, did the outcome still depend on his faith? What if Abraham had hesitated to plunge the knife into his son? Would God's plan have been aborted then? What if Abraham had stopped and said, 'This is too much, Lord. I can't handle it'?"

God has no Plan B. That is why He told Abraham, "I want you to walk perfectly," meaning *uprightly*. Scripture is clear: When God gives a promise and swears to see it fulfilled, there can be no possibility of failure. Therefore, it was not possible for Abraham to fail. Why? God was going to supply His servant with all the faith he needed. The God who revealed Himself as "He who will see to it" made sure that Abraham had everything he needed to obey His command.

God has made a covenant with us also. He said He will cause us to obey Him, and He will endue us with all the power we need to walk uprightly before Him. Because He has promised this, I believe He will do it. His very existence hinges on fulfilling these promises. It is as if He says, "I am *Jehovah Jireh,* and if I don't keep My word, My throne will collapse. I will cease to exist, and the universe will dissolve. Everything will end."

The Bible states, "They that know thy name will put their trust in thee" (Psalm 9:10) and "The name of the LORD is a strong tower: the righteous runneth into it, and is safe" (Proverbs 18:10).

The ancient Hebrews followed a practice of naming their sons with magnificently descriptive words. They believed that a good name actually gave the child power to attain its qualities. The same is true of God's names. Every revelation is a different beam of His glory, each unfolding His love and provision for His children. He wants us to run to the security of those names, fully persuaded of their meaning and power.

"For when God made promise to Abraham, because he could swear by no greater, he sware by himself, saying, Surely blessing I will bless thee, and multiplying I will multiply thee. . . . It was impossible for God to lie" (Hebrews 6:13–14, 18).

The Lord assures us, "I have committed all that I am to keep you by My grace."

two

Jehovah Rophi • Jehovah Makkeh

The Lord Who Heals You
The Lord Who Smites

At the Red Sea, Israel witnessed God's incredible destruction of the Egyptian army. The Israelites rejoiced in this victory, playing their instruments, dancing and singing: "The LORD . . . hath triumphed gloriously: the horse and his rider hath he thrown into the sea" (Exodus 15:1).

Immediately after this miraculous deliverance, Israel began a journey into the desert toward the Promised Land. In three days' time, they covered some forty miles—yet they quickly realized they had been going in circles. To their dismay, they had progressed only about twelve miles from where they had started. To make matters worse, the Israelites "found no water" (verse 22). Forty miles in the desert was more than enough time to exhaust the supply they had brought with them. In three days, they descended from the heights of praise to the depths of despair.

Then someone spotted a body of water ahead! You can imagine the wild footrace that took place to get to it. I envision the fastest and healthiest Israelites arriving first, dunking their faces into the water, taking in big gulps. A few seconds later, however, they spew the water from their mouths. They cry, "This water is bitter, undrinkable! Don't swallow it—it's rancid!"

The people trailing behind them do not believe it. They also quickly drink in big gulps, and soon they are spewing out the bitter water, too. Scripture says, "When they came to Marah, they could not drink of the waters of Marah, for they were bitter: therefore the name of it was called Marah" (verse 23).

How did God's people respond? "The people murmured against Moses, saying, What shall we drink?" (verse 24). The very same people who, just days earlier, had rejoiced in the Lord's glory were now murmuring and complaining against Him.

These people had seen God perform awesome miracles on their behalf in Egypt. First, the Lord supernaturally protected them while He devastated Egypt with plagues. Then, as the Israelites made their way toward the wilderness, God delivered them with the greatest miracle ever witnessed by man: opening a dry road through the middle of the Red Sea, with giant waves piled high on either side by strong winds.

To my mind, however, God had performed an even greater wonder. He supernaturally removed all sense of reason from the Egyptian army! How else would an entire militia rush in between such great walls of water? Any sensible soldier would have seen this wonder and thought, "Wait a minute! This is supernatural. Only God could do this. Everybody else can move ahead if they want to, but I'm not going anywhere." Yet the entire Egyptian army proceeded and was destroyed.

God's people had been absolutely defenseless against the powerful Egyptians, but they escaped Egypt successfully and survived without a single casualty. I ask you, how could any Israelite ever doubt God again after witnessing such a miracle?

Here is how: As the Israelites grew thirsty in the desert, they forgot all about God's awesome miracles on their behalf. Because they forgot, it took them less than three days to begin to doubt Him. This is true of many Christians today. Many of us have experienced miraculous wonders of God's delivering power. But then we struggle with doubt over whether or not He cares about us anymore. We know too little of our heavenly Father's character!

This is why so many believers rush all over the world looking for signs, miracles and deliverance. They are trying to get to know God through supernatural works and wonders. But nobody truly gets to know the Lord that way. The apostle Paul tells us in no uncertain terms that faith does not come through witnessing supernatural works or miracles, but through God's Word: "Faith cometh by hearing, and hearing by the word of God" (Romans 10:17).

You may ask, "What is the specific word that produces faith?" It is the word that reveals who our heavenly Father is. This is how we discover who He is—by seeing and believing for ourselves who He claims to be—and this occurs most often as God meets us in our trials.

Where Was God?

So why did God lead the Israelites to the waters of bitterness at Marah? Why did He not provide fresh water? Considering that He took control of an entire *sea* of water for them, it should have been easy for Him to change the waters at Marah! All He had to do was speak, and those waters would have been purified before the Israelites ever arrived. Why did He not do that?

The Lord brought His people to Marah in order to deal with them. He was about to begin building His wilderness church. But He could not begin that work because the camp was filled with a deadly disease that infected virtually everyone. What was that disease? The Hebrew root word for *Marah* means "corruption of bitterness." A spirit of bitterness had spread throughout Israel and it had to be dealt with.

I have often wondered how the Israelites grew so bitter. I have come to the opinion that something had happened back in Egypt that caused them to grow bitter. The roots of that bitterness had stayed alive all along, and they sprouted at the waters of Marah. The Lord simply could not lead His people another step unless this deadly disease was dealt with. So the first place He took them was to this pool of bitterness. Why? Because He wanted to use the bitter waters of Marah as a mirror for the people's hearts. As they looked into the poisonous pool, they saw a reflection of their own embittered souls.

Try to picture the scene at Marah as the people spewed out the bitter water. They must have been utterly confused. I imagine them gathering in groups within their clans, trying to figure out why God's blessing and favor had disappeared from them so quickly. They may even have tried to worship the Lord, but they probably could not muster up the spirit to do it. They were unable to quench their thirst, physically or spiritually, no matter how hard they tried.

This is exactly what bitterness does to people. It brings on confusion, a sense of God's disfavor and an inability to worship. That is the message behind this story about Israel, and I believe God wants us to see it as an illustrated sermon. He is trying to warn us about the consequences of an embittered heart.

Almost every time I talk with a Christian who is bitter, I find that person has experienced a deep disappointment with the Lord.

Perhaps this describes your life. Maybe you have bitterness that goes back to a time of crisis: marriage problems, family upheaval, a financial struggle or a tragic illness that slowly drained the life of a loved one. You were in need, hurting, crying out to God for help, believing for a miracle, doing the best you knew how—but the Lord did not seem to be there for you. Your trial dragged on, and things just got worse.

After a while you began to wonder, "How could God allow this to go on? I've loved Him, believed Him, prayed to Him. But nothing seems to change." You did not dare allow yourself to get angry with the Lord, and you made sure you did not do anything to cut yourself off from Him. But deep down, you were disappointed, and soon a seed of bitterness took root in your heart. Over time that root sprang up and blossomed. Now it continues to grow and spread in your soul.

Childhood wounds can fester into roots of bitterness. Certain traumas—abuse, beatings, molestation, abandonment—all leave their marks deep inside. They also often leave a trail of bitterness and unforgiveness in their victims' lives. I am amazed, for example, by the number of letters our ministry receives from wives who say their believing husbands hate the Christmas holiday. Many of these men were traumatized by an awful childhood experience, and now they are moody, irritable and even hateful when the holidays come around.

One woman wrote that her husband mocks her gift-giving. He will not let her put up even a Christmas wreath. She traces his bitterness back to an experience he had with his alcoholic father as a boy. One Christmas the only present he received was a broken toy his drunken father had pulled from a garbage can. While all of this boy's friends were gathering and showing off their toys, he was too embarrassed to leave the house. The experience left a deep mark on him, and he never got over it. Now he hates Christmas.

I believe that the "corruption of bitterness" in Israel began back in Egypt soon after God first sent Moses to them. When Moses arrived, the Israelites' hopes were suddenly renewed. Here was a man who claimed to be sent by the Lord, and he backed up his claims by working supernatural signs and wonders. They had spent years in bondage, enslaved in the iron furnace of Egypt. Then, when Moses spoke of God's deliverance, "the people believed: and when they heard that the LORD had visited the children of Israel, and that he had looked upon their affliction, then they bowed their heads and worshipped" (Exodus 4:31).

But the Israelites were not delivered right away. In fact, their plight grew even worse! The Egyptian taskmasters' whips came down on their backs harder than before. Pharaoh decided he would no longer supply them with the straw they needed to meet the quota of bricks. Then he increased their quotas.

You can imagine the Israelites' disappointment, both with God and with Moses. The Bible tells us, "They met Moses and Aaron, who stood in the way, as they came forth from Pharaoh: and they said unto them, The LORD look upon you, and judge; because ye have made our savour to be abhorred in the eyes of Pharaoh, and in the eyes of his servants, to put a sword in their hand to slay us" (Exodus 5:20–21).

I must confess, I have had little patience over the years with Christians who harbor bitterness. At times, I have preached hellfire-and-brimstone sermons against their debilitating sin. I did so with good reason: I have seen bitterness cause backsliding, depression, heart attacks and crippling diseases. I could never understand why the embittered people I preached to did not see what their resentment was doing to them.

Now, years later, I am awestruck as I see how tenderly the Lord dealt with the murmuring, complaining, bitter Israelites. God's gentle love toward His people, in spite of their awful condition, simply melts my heart. I am moved to ask God to give me His great love for those children of His who are burdened down with bitterness.

Here is what I find most amazing about this passage: God had given these people incredible, undeniable miracles of deliverance. Yet ever since their experience in Egypt—all through the supernatural plagues and the miraculous parting of the Red Sea—the Israelites clung to doubt, fear and unbelief. First, they did not believe Moses, the Lord's servant. Then they constantly questioned whether or not God was with them, behaving at every turn as if He had forsaken them. The Israelites' deep disappointment with the Lord was symbolized by the tiny golden idols they hid in their tents. Scripture tells us that they carried their idols with them through every mighty miracle of deliverance.

So what did God do about their idolatry? Did He chastise them or threaten to wipe them out? No, not at this time. Instead He responded by giving His people a fresh revelation of His loving nature toward them. When they got to Marah, God directed Moses to cut down a tree and cast it into the bitter waters. Then Scripture says, "When he had cast [it] into the waters, the waters were made sweet" (Exodus 15:25). We see once more that God comes to us in our crises and failures, bringing us into a new discovery of who He is and giving us another revelation of His loving kindness.

It is at Marah that we discover *Jehovah Rophi*—"the Lord who heals you." The root word for *heal* here means "to fix or mend." God told Israel,

> If thou wilt diligently hearken to the voice of the LORD thy God, and wilt do that which is right in his sight, and wilt give ear to his commandments, and keep all his statutes, I will put none of these diseases upon thee, which I have brought upon the Egyptians: for I am the LORD that healeth thee.
>
> Exodus 15:26

This is the passage that convicted me of my harshness and broke my heart. The Lord is telling His people here, "I am a God who wants to heal your diseases. I am not inclined to cast you aside. My heart is to mend you completely—body, soul and spirit. I want you to know this about My character toward you—that I am your healer."

What Do You Need to Be Healed Of?

Maybe you are bitter at God for allowing a trial to drag on longer than you thought you could bear. Or perhaps you are angry at society, or at certain individuals. Maybe you have an unforgiving spirit toward someone who has hurt you. You have convinced yourself, "I can't forgive that person. I don't care how many Scriptures they quote at me, I'm not even going to try to forgive him. No one knows what I've been through because of what was done to me. God can deal with that person. I'm taking this to my grave."

The truth is, if you allow bitterness to grow, you surely will take it to your grave. In fact, it will be attached to you as you stand before the judgment seat of Christ, because Jesus' commands are clear: There is no place for bitterness in the Christian life.

I ask you: What is the more important healing to receive—physical or spiritual? What is the point of being healed of bodily sickness—diabetes, cancer, heart disease—if we hang on to our spiritual sickness—bitterness, resentment and pride?

It does not matter what your condition is. God's nature is not to cut you off. He is telling you, "Yes, I am Jehovah God, high and holy. But I am also *Jehovah Rophi,* and I want to heal and mend you. I know you're mad at Me. Your heart has been full of bitterness toward Me for a long time. You don't want to voice it, but deep down you think, *Why did God allow this to happen to me?*

"I want you to realize that I know where your bitterness comes from. I am coming to you now in your bitter condition. You have said you cannot let go of your bitterness. You see it bringing strife into your life. It is ruining your marriage, your family. I want to pluck that bitterness out of you and heal you, so you don't have to carry it another day. Then I want you to enter into the peace and joy I am offering to you.

"Right now I am revealing something to you about My nature. I am *Jehovah Rophi,* your healer and mender, and My heart is aching to resolve your problem of bitterness. I want you back in My loving arms, full of My comfort."

Even if you harbor bitterness in your heart, you are still the Lord's possession, and He is offering you total healing. He has revealed Himself to you as *Jehovah Rophi*—your healer and mender—and He is waiting for you to trust Him. He longs to restore you to a clear conscience, to good physical health and to His divine peace and favor. He stands waiting for you now, wanting to forgive you, cleanse you and give you a new heart. Your physical healing is included in His promises, but the healing of your spirit must come first.

Grace Is Free—Not Cheap

There is a willful rejection—a stubborn holding onto hatred and unforgiveness—that provokes God's fiery indignation. I have known bitter Christians who refused to seek God's help. They rejected His offer of healing, as if He could not understand their hurt or pain. This is a very serious matter. These believers do not seem to realize that they have turned down their only possible cure. As a result, their bitterness grips them so tightly that it takes over their lives. It becomes an idol in their hearts, the very focus of their existence. It is all they can think or talk about. It begins to alienate them from family and friends. Hebrews 12:15 urges us always to be "looking diligently lest any man fail of the grace of God; lest any root of bitterness springing up trouble you, and thereby many be defiled." The Greek word for *defiled* here means "contaminated." If you hold onto bitterness, it will contaminate your family, your children, your coworkers. Whatever you touch will become infected by your bitter spirit.

Scripture warns us not to reject God's offer of healing: "If we sin willfully after that we have received the knowledge of the truth, there remaineth no more sacrifice for sins, but a certain fearful looking for of judgment and fiery indignation, which shall devour the adversaries" (Hebrews 10:26–27). In other words, if we reject His offer of healing after we have received the knowledge of *Jehovah Rophi,* we have to face His fiery indignation.

Listen to this powerful warning: "Follow peace with all men, and holiness, without which no man shall see the Lord" (Hebrews 12:14). God's Word makes it clear: If you refuse to make peace with someone by holding onto bitterness against that person, you have no chance of seeing the Lord.

The God Who Smites

Bitterness precipitates a terrible crisis. If you hold onto it, there finally comes a time when God has to quarantine you. He still loves you, of course, but He cannot allow your disease to contaminate His children around you. This kind of crisis reveals something else about God's nature: He is also *Jehovah Makkeh,* "the God who smites." He says in Ezekiel, "I will recompense thee according to thy ways and thine abominations that are in the midst of thee; and ye shall know that I am the LORD that smiteth" (Ezekiel 7:9).

You may wonder, "My Lord is a smiting God? Where's the grace in that?" I assure you, this aspect of God's nature is all about grace! In the book of Proverbs, God advises every parent to use the rod to chasten foolish, disobedient children. This discipline is meant to awaken their consciences and lead them back to wisdom. Likewise, God Himself smites His own rebellious children to return them to His holy ways. As the wise king said, "Foolishness is bound in the heart of a child; but the rod of correction shall drive it far from him" (Proverbs 22:15).

Jehovah Makkeh says to us, "I've got to discipline you in order to correct your ways. Otherwise, you are headed for tragedy. If you hold onto your bitterness, your life will start to unravel. Everything will go wrong. You will descend into utter confusion. Your home life will become chaotic. All your relationships will begin to sour and you will think everyone is against you. You will end up losing everything."

Our Lord does not want to lose any of His children. When we turn down *Jehovah Rophi's* wonderful offer, there remains no other way to healing. His only option is to become *Jehovah Makkeh,* the God who disciplines His children. This is the aspect of His nature that refuses to let us go. He says, "I cannot allow your bitterness to continue. The time has now come for it to end. I have come to you in love, mercy and great compassion, but you have rejected My offers time after time. Now I have to apply the rod to you. There has to be a smiting."

God revealed this aspect of His character to the Israelites after they had ignored His many merciful warnings. In great love and compassion, the Lord had sent His prophets and servants to warn that, if Israel continued to reject His calls to obedience, they would bring down His wrath: "They shall know that I am the LORD, and that I have not said in vain that I would do this evil unto them. . . . The rod hath blossomed, pride hath budded" (Ezekiel 6:10; 7:10). God was telling them, "Your bitterness has now taken dominion in your lives. It has blossomed into pride. Now My discipline is the only thing between you and total destruction."

God eventually smote the Israelites by sending them into captivity in Babylon. He took away their joy and peace and brought shame and confusion upon them. Yet the whole time He was after one thing—repentance. His desire was to pardon and restore His beloved people.

After that they have borne their shame, and all their trespasses whereby they have trespassed against me, when they dwelt safely in their land, and none made them afraid. When I have brought them again from the people, and gathered them out of their enemies' lands, and am sanctified in them in the sight of many nations.

Ezekiel 39:26–27

God was saying, in essence, "When you know me as *Jehovah Makkeh*—the God who smites to heal—then you will know deliverance, victory and restoration. I will smite you with discipline, to draw out your rebellion like poison from a wound."

Unless you allow *Jehovah Rophi* to heal any bitterness in your heart, you cannot grow as a Christian. If God were to heal you of some physical illness without healing the disease in your soul, He would be blessing and condoning your sin. He would be providing you with new strength to indulge your bitterness. That is why He beseeches everyone who is bitter and ill: "I want to heal you, not to smite you. Call upon Me, yield to My Spirit, and I will set you free. If you don't, you will know Me as *Jehovah Makkeh*, the God who smites. I love you, and I want you to choose healing."

If you reject God's glorious revelation as your healer—if you shrug off His offer, refusing to be mended—you will be given over to your sin. Like Korah in the Old Testament, you will bring grief upon yourself and those around you.

No matter what has caused resentment in your heart, God longs and yearns to heal your hurting soul. It is time for you to turn to *Jehovah Rophi*. Get the process started by praying, "Lord, I have carried this bitterness for too long. Now I know it is time for me to be delivered. I want to be free." He will take it the rest of the way. His Holy Spirit will bring you into a peace you have never known, filling you with singing, shouting joy. You will sleep as you have not slept in ages, because you will be back in God's favor. He will begin to work new things in your life, bringing you renewed hope—because you chose to know Him as *Jehovah Rophi*.

three

Jehovah Nissi

The Lord Our Banner

Amalek was the first nation to declare war on Israel. In turn, Amalek was the first nation that God declared war upon. Exodus describes the Lord's declaration against Amalek in the following passage:

> Then came Amalek, and fought with Israel in Rephidim. And Moses said unto Joshua, Choose us out men, and go out, fight with Amalek: tomorrow I will stand on the top of the hill with the rod of God in mine hand. So Joshua did as Moses had said to him, and fought with Amalek: and Moses, Aaron, and Hur went up to the top of the hill. And it came to pass, when

Moses held up his hand, that Israel prevailed: and when he let down his hand, Amalek prevailed. But Moses' hands were heavy; and they took a stone, and put it under him, and he sat thereon; and Aaron and Hur stayed up his hands, the one on the one side, and the other on the other side; and his hands were steady until the going down of the sun. And Joshua discomfited Amalek and his people with the edge of the sword. And the LORD said unto Moses, Write this for a memorial in a book, and rehearse it in the ears of Joshua: for I will utterly put out the remembrance of Amalek from under heaven. And Moses built an altar, and called the name of it Jehovah-nissi: for he said, Because the LORD hath sworn that the LORD will have war with Amalek from generation to generation.

Exodus 17:8–16

Two verses in this passage grab my attention; both appear toward the end of the passage: "The LORD said unto Moses . . . I will utterly put out the remembrance of Amalek from under heaven. . . . The LORD hath sworn that the LORD will have war with Amalek from generation to generation" (verses 14, 16). As I read this particular passage recently, I had to struggle to accept what God was saying. The Lord was declaring permanent war on a particular nation? How could that be?

Once I accepted that there was no other way to read the passage, my question became, Who was this nation of Amalek? What was it about these people that caused the God of the universe to go on record as saying, "I am going to do battle against you from generation to generation, and I am going to make sure you are utterly destroyed, so that your memory is erased from history"?

Obviously, the conflict had to do with more than just a local physical battle. It involved more than Moses standing on a hill with his arms in the air while Joshua led the troops in combat. We are told that Israel won this particular battle, but as we read about the people of Amalek it seems there is a deeper meaning to this passage. Indeed, Israel's war with Amalek would rage on for centuries, but I believe Israel's ongoing conflict with Amalek represents a spiritual war still being fought today. This war involves every Christian.

His Hand Was Against the Throne of God

In order for you to understand what I am driving at, it is helpful for us to examine exactly who the Amalekites were. They were descendants of Amalek—the grandson of Esau, who was Jacob's twin brother. We know Esau as the man who despised the holy things of God by selling his birthright for a meal of stew (see Genesis 25:34). The Bible says that God despised Esau because of his wickedness:

> I hated Esau, and laid his mountains and his heritage waste for the dragons of the wilderness. . . . They shall build, but I will throw down; and they shall call them, The border of wickedness, and, The people against whom the LORD hath indignation for ever.
>
> Malachi 1:3–4

As we read of God's wrath toward this nation, we need to keep in mind that the Lord has always been full of grace and mercy. Scripture tells us that He is the same yesterday, today and forever—that His nature and character never change. Therefore, God was as merciful in the Old Testament as He is in the New. Our Lord is, and always has been, a God of love and mercy. Yet He states clearly here: "My indignation will burn against this nation forever."

What exactly is happening here? I believe that God is speaking of none other than Satan and his demonic powers. You see, Amalek is a biblical representation of the devil's hostility toward Christ and His Body on earth. The margin note in an old Puritan Bible states the following as God's reason for declaring war on Amalek: "Because his hand is against the throne of God." This war continues today because Satan has never ceased his efforts to thwart God's eternal purposes. Amalek represents the devil—the enemy of the Lord, whose "hand is against the throne of God." Right up until the time of Jesus' birth Satan put his hand against God's throne by trying to destroy the lineage that would give birth to the promised Christ. The enemy did everything he possibly could to wipe out God's people.

Make no mistake, Satan knew exactly what God's promised seed was all about. He was in the Garden of Eden, listening as God told Adam that one of his descendants would come forth to crush the serpent's head. The devil also heard about what happened on Mount Moriah, when *Jehovah Jireh* provided a ram to replace Isaac as the sacrificial offering. Satan knew this animal represented Jesus, the sacrificial lamb, and he was fully aware of what God meant when he told Abraham that all humankind would be blessed by his seed. That is why Satan declared war on God's throne. He was determined to do battle against the coming of the Messiah.

Who but Satan himself could have possessed Pharaoh? This evil man decreed that every male child in Israel was to be cast into the river and drowned. The coincidence is far too strong to be accidental. Obviously Pharaoh was the mouthpiece and earthly power for a demonic spirit that was determined to kill off the Messiah's family line.

At present, Satan's warfare continues against God's seed—the Church of Jesus Christ. The devil is out to destroy anyone who inherits eternal life through the promise of the Messiah. That is why he has aimed his weapons at everyone who calls himself after Jesus' name.

Thus, the war God declared against Amalek is an everlasting conflict. Here in Exodus 17, the enemy was readying himself to engage in another attack. Satan saw Israel headed for Canaan, the Promised Land where God would settle His people. The devil knew the prophecies concerning this land. He was fully aware that this physical, geographical nation of Israel would be the place from which the Messiah would come. He knew a lineage would emerge from it—a woman giving birth to a daughter, that daughter giving birth to another daughter, and so on, until finally a descended daughter would give birth to the Christ Child. The devil was determined to do everything in his power to stop this lineage from coming to pass.

The spirit of Satan instigated and waged war on Israel for one purpose—to annihilate the seed of Abraham through which the devil's own destroyer would come. The devil was not really warring against Israel but against God Himself. As has been stated, his hand was against the throne of God. Satan was never after the Jewish people, but after the Christ whom the Jewish nation would give birth to. This was, therefore, much more than a flesh-and-blood war; it was a war between heaven and hell. That is why, in Scripture, we see God's people facing war after war with Amalek. Amalek was a Satan-controlled nation of people, and this war was a perpetual conflict waged against God by the principalities and powers of hell.

Exodus 17 is not the last we hear of the Amalekites. We see them next in Numbers 14. At that point, God told Israel to return to the wilderness. He refused to lead her into the Promised Land because of her continual sin of unbelief. He told the Israelites in no uncertain terms, "I will take your children into the land of promise, but you are not going in. You are going back to the wilderness where you will experience forty more years of despair" (see Numbers 14:34). Then, during this time of weakness for the Israelites, when the people realized their sin and decided too late to try to advance into the Promised Land, "The Amalekites came down . . . and smote them, and discomfited them" (Numbers 14:45).

The Amalekites kept rising up. We hear of them again four hundred years later, when Saul was king over Israel. God gave Saul specific instructions through the prophet Samuel, "Now go and smite Amalek, and utterly destroy all that they have, and spare them not; but slay both man and woman, infant and suckling, ox and sheep, camel and ass" (1 Samuel 15:3). God was telling Saul, "I want you to kill every man, woman and child of Amalek. I want you to destroy everything they own. Amalek is the sworn enemy of God, the one set on destroying the seed. You must wipe them out completely."

Saul won the skirmish against Amalek, but in direct disobedience to God's command, he spared King Agag and kept the best spoils from battle. When the prophet Samuel saw what Saul had done, he was grieved beyond words. He took matters into his own hands, personally picking up a sword and hacking King Agag to death. Yet even after this smiting, a remnant of Amalek survived to rise up once again.

The book of First Samuel describes an Amalekite attack on David. While David and his men were out with the Philistines, the Amalekites invaded their home village of Ziklag. The enemy raiders burned the town to the ground, took all the goods and kidnapped the families. When David and his men returned and saw what had happened, they pursued the Amalekites and overtook them. They won that battle, recovering their families and everything that had been stolen from them. But, once again, a remnant remained; four hundred young Amalekite men escaped.

Years later, during Hezekiah's reign, God's promise to wipe out Amalek was finally fulfilled. The Bible says the sons of Simeon waged war against the Amalekites, "and they smote the rest of the Amalekites that were escaped" (1 Chronicles 4:43). Although a few individuals lived, the Amalek nation was destroyed. This was the literal fulfillment of Moses' prophecy that God would "put out the remembrance of Amalek from under heaven."

The Amalekite Spirit

The spirit that possessed the Amalekites continued to torment God's people. Even though Amalek had few surviving descendants, an Amalekite spirit had spread around the world. We see this demonstrated several generations later when Haman, a Persian official, rose to power and plotted to wipe out Israel. The amazing thing about this story is that Haman was an Amalekite, a distant descendant of an Amalekite king named Agag. (All of the Amalekite kings took the name Agag. The name represented an office, the way the title of *pharaoh* represented the leader's role in Egypt.) Scripture calls Haman "the Jews' enemy" (Esther 3:10). Using subtle devices, this evil man seduced a pagan king into signing the death warrant of the Jewish people. Scripture says, "The letters were sent by posts into all the king's provinces, to destroy, to kill, and to cause to perish, all Jews, both young and old, little children and women, in one day" (verse 13).

I ask you, does this sound like the mad crusade of a single Jew-hater, a descendant of the remnant of the Amalekites? Was Haman personally going to take revenge on an entire race of people because, as this story tells us, one Jew, Mordecai, would not bow to him? No, this was the same, age-old spiritual conflict. It was a war against God's throne—one more attempt to abort the coming Savior who would deliver God's people from Satan's power. I believe that Haman was merely an instrument of the devil. The satanic spirit of Amalek that possessed this man declared once more, "I am going to kill off every Jewish man, woman and child. I will wipe them off the face of the earth entirely. Then there won't be any chance of a Messiah coming to destroy me."

But God had His own human instrument in place to crush Satan's plan. He raised up a single person among that generation, a young woman named Esther, to accomplish His eternal purpose. Esther was the niece of Mordecai, a Jew who refused to bow to pagan royalty. This godly young woman instructed every Jew in the land to fast and pray for three days. You probably know the rest of the story: The Lord gave Esther the king's ear, and Haman's diabolical plan was exposed. Not one Jew was killed—and Haman ended up being hanged on the very gallows he had built to execute Mordecai.

Lessons from Rephidim

Now let us take another look at the battle of Rephidim, which Israel fought with the Amalekites soon after her miraculous escape through the Red Sea. I pray that God will open your spiritual eyes to see what the Holy Spirit wants to teach about our own spiritual warfare through these stories of the Israelites and the Amalekites. I believe the lesson is urgent. Peter reminds us, "Your adversary the devil, as a roaring lion, walketh about, seeking whom he may devour" (1 Peter 5:8). Likewise, Paul tells us, "Now all these things happened unto them for ensamples: and they are written for our admonition, upon whom the ends of the world are come" (1 Corinthians 10:11). And: "Now these things were our examples, to the intent we should not lust after evil things, as they also lusted" (1 Corinthians 10:6).

I believe Paul is saying that all of these things—the wars, battles and conflicts—happened to Israel for our instruction. Scripture has recorded them to warn us about the spiritual battles we face. We learn important New Testament truths about Christ by studying the Old Testament aspects of Jehovah's nature.

So, what are these lessons we are to learn? What is the Holy Spirit saying to us?

We Face Amalek Daily

The primary lesson is that we are engaged in the same ongoing spiritual battle. Paul writes, "We wrestle not against flesh and blood, but against principalities, against powers, against the rulers of the darkness of this world, against spiritual wickedness in high places" (Ephesians 6:12).

Amalek's first attacks on Israel were a type of guerrilla warfare in the wilderness. They blindsided the Israelites at their points of weakness with quick sneak attacks. For example, they sent soldiers to sneak up on Israel from behind while they were traveling. That way they could quietly kill off the old, weak and infirm who could not keep up with the others.

Finally, Moses told Joshua, "Choose us out men, and go out, fight with Amalek" (Exodus 17:9). Joshua quickly put together a makeshift army of men with very little battle experience. These were shepherds and brick makers, not soldiers! They had few weapons or shields, and no chariots. Their enemy had all of these things, plus years of training. Certainly, the odds were against Israel.

Just Keep Swinging

This is our second lesson: When the enemy comes against us like a flood, what does God tell His people to do? "Go in faith and fight, no matter what the odds." Our options during such times are clear: We can either trust in God's Spirit to raise up a banner on our behalf, or we can surrender to unbelief, giving in to the enemy and becoming his slaves.

What do you usually do in such a moment? Do you sigh, give in to despair and say, "This battle is too big for me"? That is the reaction of many Christians today. They give up, thinking they just cannot handle the conflict anymore. Yet our Lord clearly tells us, "I want you to fight the good fight of faith."

It is important for us to take a closer look at the men Joshua was leading into war. These men were not only inexperienced—they were the most messed-up bunch of soldiers you could find. Shortly before, these same men had been ready to stone Moses because they had run out of water. They accused him of bringing them out of Egypt to kill them and their families. Then they accused God of abandoning them, saying, "Is the LORD among us, or not?" (Exodus 17:7). Tell me, how can you go into battle for the Lord if you do not believe God is with you? This crew was made up of murmuring, unbelieving, miserable complainers. They wavered constantly between weak faith and stifling unbelief.

What a weak army God used to fight the devil! Keep in mind, the Lord had every right to destroy these ungrateful people or simply abandon them. Then He could have raised up another, more faithful people, but He did nothing of the sort. Instead He appointed these men as His army and told them, "Go and fight."

Today we are often no better than the Israelites were. We murmur and complain. We see God supplying our needs and blessing our lives, but when a crisis comes we panic, crying out, "Where's God? Why is He letting me go through this? I had it easier when I was a sinner!" We may talk frequently about our growing faith, sing God's praises in church and raise our hands in glorious worship. But the moment the enemy comes against us, we crumble and cry, "Oh, Lord, this is too much for me."

What a marvelous testimony of grace it is that God uses such weak, unworthy people to be soldiers in His army! An even greater wonder of grace is that He makes us more than conquerors against our enemy!

Remember Our Intercessor

As Joshua led these wavering men into combat with the Amalekites, Moses led Aaron and Hur up a hill overlooking the battlefield. Moses stood up in full view of the conflict below, holding up a wooden rod. "And it came to pass, when Moses held up his hand, that Israel prevailed: and when he let down his hand, Amalek prevailed" (Exodus 17:11).

What is this scene all about? What lesson should it teach us about doing battle in God's army? Most commentaries suggest Moses' upraised hands represent intercession and prayer. In other words, as long as he raised his hands, he was interceding—and as long as he interceded, the battle went in Israel's favor. So another lesson here is about our need for prayer and intercession in doing battle against Satan. Jesus Himself spoke on this subject. When the disciples were unable to cast out a demon, Christ told them, "This kind goeth not out but by prayer and fasting" (Matthew 17:21).

I see another meaning in this passage, however, and I believe it goes beyond the subject of our own prayer lives. I suggest that the Lord wants to reveal the following to us: This story is about Jesus—about the power and victory of His cross and about the intercession He makes for us in glory.

Moses must have been fully aware that his actions were somehow representative of the coming Messiah. He later prophesied, "The LORD thy God will raise up unto thee a Prophet from the midst of thee, of thy brethren, like unto me; unto him ye shall hearken" (Deuteronomy 18:15).

We see this demonstrated in the image of Moses carrying a wooden rod up the hill. This is another clear foreshadowing of Christ's journey up the hill of Golgotha. Moses' rod here represents the cross of Christ. Likewise, Moses' raising of his hands atop the hill represents the prayers and supplications of Christ, our High Priest.

As we envision Moses standing at the top of the hill, holding up the rod, we see yet another foreshadowing of Christ. This was a picture of Jesus on the cross at Calvary—looking down upon humanity and beholding the great conflict being waged by Satan against His Body.

Moreover, whenever the Israelites looked up and saw Moses holding the rod, the battle turned in their favor. This points to Jesus' day, when Christ said, "I, if I be lifted up from the earth, will draw all men unto me" (John 12:32).

As the battle at Rephidim wore on, "Moses' hands were heavy" (Exodus 17:12). We see this same heaviness at Gethsemane, where

Jesus' work of intercession grew heavy under the burden of man's sin. Matthew writes, "Then cometh Jesus . . . and saith unto the disciples, Sit ye here, while I go and pray yonder . . . and [He] began to be sorrowful and very heavy" (Matthew 26:36–37).

Yet another parallel to Christ occurs as Aaron and Hur try to aid Moses. "They took a stone, and put it under him, and he sat thereon" (Exodus 17:12). Evidently, from the moment Moses sat down, the battle swung completely toward the Israelites' favor. Now note what Hebrews says about Jesus: "When he had by himself purged our sins, [he] sat down on the right hand of the Majesty on high. . . . But this man, after he had offered one sacrifice for sins for ever, sat down on the right hand of God; from henceforth expecting till his enemies be made his footstool" (Hebrews 1:3; 10:12–13).

Finally, the rod that Moses held up provided the Israelites with a supernatural surge of power. Ultimately, that power led them to victory over the Amalekites: "Joshua discomfited Amalek and his people with the edge of the sword" (Exodus 17:13). The Israelites' sudden strength must have totally confused the well-armed, well-trained Amalekites. Once again, we see an obvious parallel to the kind of supernatural power given to God's people in the New Testament. Paul writes, "The preaching of the cross is to them that perish foolishness; but unto us which are saved it is the power of God" (1 Corinthians 1:18).

Please do not misunderstand. I am not saying that when Moses held up the rod, he thought, *This represents the cross our Lord will die on.* Nor am I saying that when Moses sat down, he reasoned, *This foretells the time when the Messiah will be seated at the right hand of God, in full authority.* No, the battle Moses saw before him was real, with men fighting and dying, left and right. It was a very present conflict, having to do with flesh-and-blood Israelites. Yet through this battle, God was trying to show His people that if they would trust His banner over them (represented by the upraised rod), He would lead them to victory.

As we have noted, of course, Israel's victory over Amalek was not complete at this point. Some of the Amalekites escaped to regroup and attack Israel again. But this entire passage evokes the image of Christ to come, when the victory over Satan would be complete.

Moses built an altar there and called it *Jehovah Nissi*—Hebrew for "the Lord my banner, the Lord my ensign" (see Exodus 17:15). This meant, in effect, "We have won the battle here today, and we cannot forget that we were victorious because we serve *Jehovah Nissi*—the Lord, our banner. This victory had nothing to do with our strength or ability or any great works we promised to do for God. We did nothing to earn the Lord's favor today. God Himself is our banner—and our victory is totally the work of His hand."

Lessons from the Prophets

In the passage from Exodus that we read at the beginning of this chapter, Moses tied the revelation of *Jehovah Nissi's* name to every succeeding generation: "Moses built an altar, and called the name of it Jehovah-nissi: for he said, Because the LORD hath sworn that the LORD will have war with Amalek from generation to generation" (Exodus 17:15–16). Two things are obvious from this passage: First, the revelation of *Jehovah Nissi's* name has to do with the spiritual warfare God declared against Amalek. Second, this warfare will continue from generation to generation.

From Abraham onward, in both the Old and New Testaments, *Jehovah Nissi,* the Lord our banner, is declared. The prophets and righteous servants looked forward to His coming, saying, "This is the one who will be our banner." Paul looked back to Him, saying, "Everything in the Old Testament is about Jesus. Every battle, every conflict, every war we read about here gives us another revelation of who He is."

Look at this extraordinary prophecy of Christ by Isaiah, declaring *Jehovah Nissi* to a new generation:

> There shall come forth a rod out of the stem of Jesse, and a Branch shall grow out of his roots: and the spirit of the LORD shall rest upon him, the spirit of wisdom and understanding, the spirit of counsel and might, the spirit of knowledge and of the fear of the LORD; and shall make him of quick understanding in the fear of the LORD: and he shall not judge after the sight of his eyes, neither reprove after the hearing of his ears: But with righteousness shall he judge the poor, and reprove with equity for the meek of the earth: and he shall smite the earth with the rod of his mouth, and with the breath of his lips shall he slay the wicked.
>
> Isaiah 11:1–4

The rod of Jesse whom Isaiah mentions is Jesus, who is also called "the son of David." Isaiah was declaring Christ to be the banner whom the world would rally under.

Jesus Himself told His disciples, "Your forefathers longed to see all the things you see Me doing. They saw Me only in shadow, but you see Me in reality" (see Matthew 13:17).

Our forefathers did not receive the promise, but they did embrace its future fulfillment by faith. Hebrews tells us, "These all died in faith, not having received the promises, but having seen them afar off, and were persuaded of them, and embraced them, and confessed that they were strangers and pilgrims on the earth" (Hebrews 11:13).

Jesus alone provides us with victory over Amalek and with sweet rest and peace.

Fighting the Good Fight

In my opinion, Moses is telling today's Church of Jesus Christ, "*Jehovah Nissi* delivered us from the demonic power of Amalek, and as long as the spirit of Amalek continues to rage against

God's people, *Jehovah Nissi* will be your banner. He will cover you through every future generation, down to the very end of time. Always look, therefore, to *Jehovah Nissi*. This is our secret to victory—the revelation of our Lord's nature toward us."

You may wonder, "Didn't Jesus end the battle with His victory on the cross? Wasn't His victory total and complete? After all, He was raised up by the Spirit's resurrection power, breaking the bonds of death. When He ascended to heaven, He was beyond the devil's reach forever. The victory was, is and forever will be Christ's. Doesn't that mean the battle should be over?"

Yes, Jesus' victory on the cross was complete, total and absolute. But we, His Church, are still in a battle. You see, while Jesus sits victoriously as Head in heaven at the right hand of the Father, beyond Satan's reach, we remain His Body here on earth. The New Testament clearly states that we face a roaring lion who seeks to devour us. We are still, therefore, engaged in warfare. We have to battle daily with the principalities and powers of darkness—because the devil wars against Christ in us. This is why Paul instructs us to take up our spiritual weapons by putting on the whole armor of God (see Ephesians 6). We are to fight the good fight of faith against the enemy who is still alive and at work on earth. The victory Jesus won becomes our own as we resist the devil by faith.

Let's Get Personal

So, I ask you: Is Amalek attacking you right now? Are you experiencing some kind of spiritual warfare? Are you battling a temptation or desire? Is your enemy trying to lull you into loving pleasure more than you love God? Are you plagued by guilt, fear or condemnation? Is your marriage or family under attack? Are you sensing the enemy's tactics against you in your job or career? Has he come against you personally with depression, weariness or a strange, inexplicable restlessness?

It is vital for you to have a true biblical understanding of what is going on in your life right now. You are in the midst of warfare, whether you want to be or not. Once you adopt this biblical view of warfare, your perspective on everything will change.

First, you must understand that the devil is not mad at you personally. Ultimately, his battle is not with you. His hand is set against the throne of God. When Satan comes against you like a flood, therefore, he is not just trying to get you to become a fornicator or thief or alcoholic or selfish heathen. That is not his real goal in trying to hurt you. Rather, he is attacking you for one reason: because you are Christ's heritage—and it is that holy seed he is after.

You see, Satan is still in a war against Christ. Since he knows that he lost his battle against Jesus on earth, he now tries to hurt Him through His Church. That is the only way Satan expects ever to win against the throne of God—by wiping out all of Christ's seed from the earth. The devil believes that if he can destroy every Christian, he can still overcome. That is why he seduces and tempts your sinful human nature—because you have come under the banner of Christ. So, yes, you are in a battle, but it is not your battle. It is a battle between the devil and the throne of God.

Satan has one simple strategy against you in this battle: He wants to convince you to give up on Jesus. That is why he tries to terrify you, to cause you to faint in your faith—so you will distrust Christ and desert Him. He wants to make you run from the battle, to leave the Lord's army and stop being His representative on earth. This is how the enemy plans to destroy the seed—by killing off Christ's army, one soldier at a time.

It is a tragedy that many believers have already deserted Jesus. They say, "I tried, but the battle was too hard. I hoped, I prayed, I did everything I thought I should. All along I thought the Holy Spirit would be there for me. But in my hour of temptation, He was nowhere to be found. The battle was beyond me."

That is Satan's primary purpose in his battle against you: to totally discourage you. He wants to get you focused on the awfulness of your sin, persuaded you are powerless to resist temptation and convinced that God has left you alone so that you will no longer look to Christ's victory on the cross.

This is why God gave us this word:

> O Israel, ye approach this day unto battle against your enemies: let not your hearts faint, fear not, and do not tremble, neither be ye terrified because of them; for the LORD your God is he that goeth with you, to fight for you against your enemies, to save you.
>
> Deuteronomy 20:3–4

King David always knew that the battle was not his. He knew it rested completely in God's hands. That is why he could stand without fear as he faced the giant Goliath. David said, "The battle isn't mine—it's the Lord's. You have not defied me, Goliath—you have defied the living God. You have put your hand against His throne. And now you have to face Him on the battlefield" (see 1 Samuel 17:36, 47).

A Banner of Saving Grace

Jehovah Nissi—Christ my banner—means He is the captain of my salvation. Because of the revelation of the name *Jehovah Nissi*, we can declare the following:

> I am kept by the rod upon the hill and the blood that was shed there. I am also kept by my Lord's intercession for me at the right hand of the Father. He has wiped out every one of my sins—annihilating them and removing them from my life completely. Moreover, I have the promise of His blood purging every sin I will ever commit. All I have to do is come to the rod—to repent and look upon Christ and His victory on the cross. As long as I live, I have His complete forgiveness. As long as I trust

in the power of His blood, I am empowered by the Holy Ghost. *Jehovah Nissi* is Christ my intercessor.

The prophet we see standing on the hill with His hands raised up is our risen Christ. His banner over us is intercession. Right now, He stands before the very throne of God, pleading our case: "But this man, because he continueth ever, hath an unchangeable priesthood. Wherefore he is able also to save them to the uttermost that come unto God by him, seeing he ever liveth to make intercession for them" (Hebrews 7:24–25).

Is your heart guilt-ridden, riding low under a burden of condemnation? Embrace the word of the Lord: "Who is he that condemneth? It is Christ that died, yea rather, that is risen again, who is even at the right hand of God, who also maketh intercession for us. Who shall separate us from the love of Christ?" (Romans 8:34–35).

The name *Jehovah Nissi* has meant two important things in my life:

1. *The cross.* This is something Jesus has already done for me. In all my present battles, I am able to look to His victory on the cross. He has made provision to cover me forever in His blood, canceling out all my present sins whenever I repent and cry out to Him.
2. *Intercession.* This is something Jesus does for me now. My banner is seated at the right hand of the Father, acting as my High Priest and intercessor. When He sat down there, He did so to pray for me. I trust fully in the power and effectiveness of His prayers for me.

It does not matter what your spiritual battle is—it rests in the Lord's hands. He wants you to place that battle completely under His blood. Then remind yourself, and the devil, that *Jehovah Nissi* is praying for you. Jesus told us that He prayed for His disciples, and those prayers protected every one of His followers while He was on earth. "I pray for them . . . which thou hast given me . . . those that thou gavest me I have kept, and none of them is lost" (John 17:9, 12). If our Lord's prayers prevailed while He was on earth, how much more will His prayers be effective for us in glory? He has already assured us, "None of My children will be lost."

Who can condemn you? What enemy can separate you from the love of Christ? There is none. You are victorious—because *Jehovah Nissi* is praying for you.

Be careful, then, not to use the Lord's love and grace to excuse sin. He is now praying for you to turn from all your iniquities and enter the reality of His power over the dominion of sin. He has promised to infuse you with the power of the Holy Ghost to live an overcoming life.

four

Jehovah Tsebaioth

The Lord of Hosts

Those who declare war on their sin and unbelief may find that the Lord has reserved for them a powerful revelation. These believers have decided they are going into the Promised Land, no matter what it costs them. They are willing to do battle with anything that stands between them and the fullness of God's covenant promises.

Joshua was just such a believer. He was determined with all his heart, soul, mind and strength to go the distance with God. This man was born into a generation of compromise, bitterness and rebellion. Yet Joshua stepped out from among his peers and set a standard of his own. By his life he stated, "I refuse to be like this compromising crowd. I have a hunger in my heart for God, and I am not going to allow this generation's filth and unbelief to corrupt me. I know that I have a lot to learn about my Lord. He has made many covenant promises to His people and I intend to lay hold of every one of those promises. This starts today, and there is no going back for me. I have set my heart to enter all the way into God's promised rest. I am determined to resist, sacrifice, obey and surrender. I will do anything necessary to bring down all strongholds that stand between me and total victory."

Here is what the Lord showed this believer:

> It came to pass, when Joshua was by Jericho, that he lifted up his eyes and looked, and, behold, there stood a man over against him with his sword drawn in his hand: and Joshua went unto him, and said unto him, Art thou for us, or for our adversaries? And he said, Nay; but as captain of the host of the LORD am I now come. And Joshua fell on his face to the earth, and did worship, and said unto him, What saith my lord unto his servant? And the captain of the LORD's host said unto Joshua, Loose thy shoe from off thy foot; for the place whereon thou standest is holy. And Joshua did so.

> Joshua 5:13–15

What a powerful revelation! In this scene, the Lord revealed Himself to Joshua as *Jehovah Tsebaioth*—the Lord of hosts. As He stood before His humbled servant, He wielded a sword and He commanded an army of angels, heavenly soldiers who stood ready to take up the fight for Israel.

For me, Joshua represents a holy remnant who are living in this last hour. Like him, these lovers of Jesus are determined to go all the way with the Lord. Their hearts' sole cry is to walk in holiness, worthy of Christ. They yearn to be free of every false thing, every stronghold of iniquity, every dominion of besetting sins. They refuse to allow anything in their lives that might drag them from that determination. They want nothing of the greed, fame and pleasures of this world. Like Joshua, they have crossed a line. They have left behind the world and its allurements, once and for all. They are passing over the Jordan to follow the Lord into the fullness of His covenant promises.

Joshua was the leader of a new generation in Israel. The previous generation ended up dying in the wilderness because of their unbelief. Those miserable people lived under a curse until every last one of them died. But this hungry new Joshua Company began to seek God. They were ready to declare war on anything that stood in the way of their entering into the fullness of the land God had promised them.

God reveals Himself as the Lord of hosts only to those who set their hearts and minds to walk before Him in purity. He does not give this revelation to people who only want their sins forgiven and to make it to heaven someday. The lukewarm, the halfhearted and the worldly believer will never know *Jehovah Tsebaioth*.

Tragically, a majority of Christians today are not even aware of their need for *Jehovah Tsebaioth*. This is because they are not doing battle, not seeking victory, not moving forward in their walk with Christ. Instead, they have made peace with the sins that grip them. Why would the Lord send His heavenly army to help believers who are not even willing to take up the fight?

Four Requirements for Victory

Just before Moses died, he received a supernatural vision of the Lord. In this vision, he saw God riding "upon the heaven in thy help, and in his excellency on the sky" (Deuteronomy 33:26). Joshua's vision was a clearer picture of this image of the Lord, who was leading an army, a host of heavenly beings waiting to receive their next assignment.

I believe the revelation Joshua received of *Jehovah Tsebaioth* is meant for every devoted lover of Jesus today. Right now, hosts of heavenly beings are riding through the heavens on our behalf, waiting to receive their next assignment to fight for us. They are stationed all over the world—a troop here, a battalion there. They are the unseen forces of heaven, fighting against principalities and powers of darkness.

I say to every lover of Jesus: We had better believe that we need God's heavenly hosts fighting on our behalf. We cannot possibly combat hell's forces with any amount of human strength. Like the hungry young believers in Joshua's day, the Joshua Company of this last hour cannot move forward into God's promised victory without experiencing four things. These four things are required of everyone who would lay hold fully of God's covenant promises.

1. We Have to Cross over the Jordan.

"The priests that bare the ark of the covenant of the LORD stood firm on dry ground in the midst of the Jordan, and all the Israelites passed over on dry ground, until all the people were passed clean over Jordan" (Joshua 3:17).

The Jordan River has great significance in the life of every Christian. Like Israel, we come to our own Jordan crossings when we tire of the dead, dry Christianity we see all around us. When we grow weary of the backslidden condition of the church—sick of the worldliness, unbelief and idolatry running rampant in churches that grieve God's Spirit— we have reached the Jordan. When we are totally disgusted with the wilderness of old religious systems, we have reached the Jordan. When the Holy Spirit has stirred our hearts, and we realize that we will never be satisfied with the kind of life led by our carnal, pleasure-seeking society, we have reached the Jordan. If, as we turn inward to examine our own spiritual conditions we are troubled by what we see there also, then we have truly reached the Jordan.

At the Jordan, we cry out, "Lord, I have had enough of this backslidden, ineffectual Christianity. I want to be delivered from the power of sin and materialism. I want a heart that is pure and holy before You. I refuse just to drift along in these last days, satisfied with a lukewarm spirit. I want to be a light for Jesus amid this wicked generation. I am determined to seek You, Lord, and to obtain Your strength. I want to go all the way with You, no matter what the cost."

Have you set your heart to follow Jesus in this way? Have you followed the Joshua Company to the bank of the Jordan? If you have, then you must face this fact: You have come to a place of death. When you cross the Jordan, you undergo a death to this world and everything in it.

Jesus is our example. As Jesus was being baptized in the Jordan, the heavenly Father declared, "Behold My Son, in whom I am well pleased. He is Mine and He represents Me fully." The same happens with us when we undergo death to this world. As we come up on the other side, the Holy Spirit identifies us as God's own, declaring, "This is My beloved son, My beloved daughter." He hears our cries for the Spirit to empower us. He sees us seeking Him for an overcoming life, freedom from all chains of sin, lust and pride. He responds by drawing us into covenant with Him.

Make no mistake about it: Crossing the Jordan is a declaration of war. You are committing to do battle with every sin that stands between you and God's fullness. You are crossing a line that says, "I won't live with this lust anymore. I am walking toward Jesus, toward holiness and purity of heart. I am not looking back. I declare all-out war on this stronghold."

When the Israelites crossed the Jordan toward the Promised Land, they went on the offensive. They knew that as soon as they got to the other side, they would be in enemy territory.

When they arrived, word spread quickly among their enemies: "The Israelites are in the land, and they mean business. They are no longer wandering around aimlessly in the wilderness. Their God is once again doing wonders in their midst, and they are determined to take dominion."

This was quite a change. Before Israel crossed the Jordan the enemy strongholds there had remained unchallenged for years. The Hittites, Canaanites and Jebusites all had heard about Israel's wanderings in the wilderness and they were not afraid. The word about Israel was, "These people are harmless. They have been talking about taking the offensive for forty years now, but they are drifters, hopelessly aimless. All we have seen them do is murmur and complain. They're all talk. They don't live up to what they say they believe. They don't pray to their God anymore. They must not even believe He exists. We have nothing to worry about from these people."

Up to this time, the city of Jericho had its gates open for trade. People came and went as they pleased, unafraid of the Israelites' presence on the wilderness side of the Jordan. The Canaanites laughed at the Israelites, considering the threat of their possessing the land a joke. But the moment Israel crossed the river, everything changed. The inhabitants of Canaan sensed something serious going on with God's people. Suddenly the Israelites were in the Promised Land and Jericho promptly shut its gates. Within days, they saw the Israelites marching fearlessly around the walls of their city. The Bible says, "All the inhabitants of the land faint because of you" (Joshua 2:9). Israel's presence was now totally intimidating.

What an incredible turnaround in such a short amount of time! Think about it: As Israel's soldiers marched around the base of the city, they were easy targets for the enemy's fiery arrows. Yet the men of Jericho never tried to attack. Why? Apparently they were so afraid they did not even dare to draw their bows. They simply had no courage left: "As soon as we had heard these things, our hearts did melt, neither did there remain any more courage in any man, because of you: for the LORD your God, he is God in heaven above, and in earth beneath" (verse 11).

What about your personal Jericho? Have you tried to coexist with your own stronghold of sin, wandering around aimlessly in a spiritual wilderness? Has the devil mocked you and made jokes about you and your walk with Christ?

Declare war! Commit yourself to God and you will have crossed your Jordan. The enemy knows when you are committed. James tells us, "Resist the devil, and he will flee from you" (James 4:7). When the enemy sees you coming at him, marching boldly on the offensive, he will retreat in fear and shut the gates behind him, just as he did at Jericho.

Perhaps you have lived with a besetting sin for years: adultery, pornography, unbelief, stubbornness, rebellion, bitterness. Over time, the devil will have used that one weakness to build up a stronghold in your soul. He will have done his best to build walls around that area of your heart—walls to keep out the conviction of the Holy Spirit.

Year after year, those walls grow thicker and stronger. Now there is simply no way you can humanly cast out such a stronghold. You need divine, unseen power to work away on those walls for you. You need *Jehovah Tsebaioth* to do the supernatural work of tearing them down.

That work begins the moment you stand up and declare war on your sin. You have to see your habits as a spiritual battlefield. Your Jordan is simply a decision you make to take victory over the devil—a decision to surrender to God. By doing so, you become a warrior on the offensive. You declare that you are no longer a wimp, that you are now unwilling to be a slave to Satan's devices and delusions. You renounce all ties to this filthy world. You call on the Holy Ghost to empower you to wage war against all sin in your life. You declare, "I'm crossing a line and I'm not going back. By the help of the Holy Spirit, I am going to live a righteous, clean, holy life. It does not matter how wicked and vile the world around me becomes. I want to be part of God's Joshua Company." With this single resolve, you strike fear in the heart of Satan and all his hellish hosts.

This leads us to the second requirement of everyone who would go on to obtain God's promised victory.

2. We Have to Face the Sharp Knife of Circumcision.

I remember an old Gospel song from my childhood called, "This Is Like Heaven to Me." The chorus goes, "Oh, this is like heaven to me, yes, this is like heaven to me. I have crossed over Jordan to Canaan's fair land, and this is like heaven to me." Whoever wrote that song never read Joshua 5. When the Israelites got to the other side of the Jordan, it was anything but heaven for them.

At first, Joshua's fresh young warriors probably thought they were in heaven. After all, they had finally made it into the Promised Land. I imagine them falling on their faces and kissing the ground. Now they were ready for a fight, crying, "Let's go. We're going to tear down that walled city, brick by brick. We've got what it takes. And the Lord is on our side. Let us at 'em."

Yet while these soldiers may have been pumping themselves up, Joshua sat by himself, quietly sharpening knives. He knew that enthusiasm and excitement alone were not going to win any war. There would be a time to shout, but now was not the time. First these men had to face the knife of circumcision: "At that time the LORD said unto Joshua, Make thee sharp knives, and circumcise again the children of Israel the second time. And Joshua made him sharp knives, and circumcised the children of Israel at the hill of the foreskins" (Joshua 5:2–3).

Why would God require these men to be circumcised at this time? What was this scene all about? Down through the centuries, an entire theology has been developed regarding the meaning of circumcision. Countless sermons have been preached on the subject and many books have been written about it. Simply put, circumcision is an outward act that signifies something taking place in the heart. "Circumcise therefore the foreskin of your heart, and be no more stiffnecked" (Deuteronomy 10:16). "Circumcision is that of the heart, in the spirit, and not in the letter" (Romans 2:29). "In whom also ye are circumcised with the circumcision made without hands, in putting off the body of the sins of the flesh by the circumcision of Christ" (Colossians 2:11).

These soldiers' circumcisions at Gilgal involved cutting flesh, but they also illustrated a spiritual commitment. We know this from Moses' speech to Israel before he died. Moses foresaw the entire event of circumcision at Gilgal. He envisioned the gathering of God's people, ready to go to battle against Jericho. He spoke prophetically to them about undergoing this significant rite:

> The LORD thy God will bring thee into the land which thy fathers possessed, and thou shalt possess it; and he will do thee good, and multiply thee above thy fathers. And the LORD thy God will circumcise thine heart, and the heart of thy seed, to love the LORD thy God with all thine heart, and with all thy soul, that thou mayest live.
>
> Deuteronomy 30:5–6

The circumcision of Israel's soldiers here had to do with spiritual warfare. It signified the end of all confidence in the flesh. God knew these men's hearts were full of enthusiasm. He saw them chomping at the bit to tear down the satanic stronghold of Jericho, but the Lord commanded Joshua to put the knife to all of their posturing and self-confidence. They were to cut off all trust in their human strength.

I can assure you, the next day these soldiers were not shouting, dancing and singing, "This is like heaven to me." On the contrary, they were groaning in pain. God rendered them absolutely impotent. For a short season, they were helpless, utterly useless as soldiers. Scripture tells us, "They abode in their places in the camp, till they were whole" (Joshua 5:8).

What was God teaching His people here? He wanted them to see how completely powerless they were in the flesh. He wanted their impotence to sink deeply into their hearts, to convince them they could be saved only by faith in Him. God intentionally brought them to this place of utter weakness, because He wanted to prove Himself strong on their behalf.

If enemy scouts had spied on Israel at that moment, they would have seen the Israelites lying scattered about in absolute weakness. Once again, Israel's enemies could have attacked them and put an end to the entire warfare. Why didn't they? Why didn't the devil move in at that moment and destroy Israel in their weakened condition? I believe that he was not allowed to, because heaven's unseen forces were at work protecting God's people. If the Lord had opened the Israelites' eyes, they would have seen fierce spiritual activity going on around them: fiery horses racing over the hills and angels influencing kings and leaders. These heavenly beings were battling down principalities and putting fear into people's hearts all across the land.

Through it all God wanted to prove to Israel that He alone was their defense. He wanted to convince them, "This isn't your battle. Victory will never come through your own hands. It will not happen through your muscle, might or power. It will come to you only through My Spirit."

We can sing all the choruses we know about walking over the devil. We can shout and rail against the enemy, shake our fists at him and try to bind him in Jesus' name, but it is all meaningless noise until we come under the knife of circumcision. All our skills, willpower and boasting are useless unless we cast our self-confidence onto the hill of foreskins.

Paul writes, "For we are the circumcision, which worship God in the spirit, and rejoice in Christ Jesus, and have no confidence in the flesh" (Philippians 3:3). The apostle then makes a powerful statement: "I have suffered the loss of all things, and do count them but dung, that I may win Christ" (verse 8). What was Paul referring to here, when he said he gave up "all things" and cast them onto the hill of foreskins? He was talking about his great education, his human intellect, his own righteousness—his trust in his flesh. He said that he counted all of these things to be nothing more than dung, headed for the sewer. He was saying, "I have learned that I absolutely have to do away with confidence in the flesh—and that is a very painful lesson to learn."

Some time ago I heard a minister on the radio preaching about persistence. He said, "If you really want to please the Lord, you just have to try harder."

No! He got it all wrong. You could spend your whole life trying harder and you would fail at every turn. You could determine to do everything I have mentioned so far—draw a line, cross the Jordan and leave behind all your lukewarmness and flirtation with the world—but you would still end up in defeat and despair. Determination is not enough. New resolve is not enough. Getting fed up with your wilderness of sin is not enough. Your will—your enthusiasm and human strength—has to be broken. You have to embrace fully the fact that you are powerless to bring down your personal Jericho. You need an army—an unseen, supernatural, heavenly force—to fight the evil powers that have dug into your stronghold.

Our ministry received a letter from a dear Christian housewife whose husband abandoned her, leaving her to raise six children alone. The couple had been married for 25 years, and this wife had spent all that time caring for the children and their household needs. Now, with her husband gone, she had no job skills, no means of income and six needy children to feed. Her situation seemed hopeless. She was absolutely panic-stricken.

This woman had nowhere to turn but to the Lord, and she made up her mind she would trust God fully for all her needs. He would have to be her husband, her provider and her counselor. So, first, she made sure that she took all her children to church regularly. When the cupboard was bare, she prayed until God provided groceries. This continued for years—and her needs were supplied at every turn. She wrote, "There were times we had to kneel and ask God to send us our next meal. But, in all those years, the Lord has always been faithful to provide for us. In fact, He's been better to my family than I ever could have imagined."

Today, every one of that woman's children is serving the Lord. Her oldest just married a wonderful man who is entering full-time ministry.

How did she get through it all? She did it by casting herself completely into the arms of her heavenly Father. She refused to put her confidence in man or in her own strength.

Try to imagine all the heavenly activity surrounding this family's comings and goings. I can just see the heavenly hosts moving here and there, giving divine directions to people all around her. They directed one Christian family to take her a bag of groceries. They instructed another to fill her car with gas. They told her pastor to involve her family in church activities. God simply would not allow the people in this woman's church community to sleep until they fulfilled what He prompted their hearts to do for her. The Lord had heavenly principalities working on her behalf everywhere. This is exactly how she made it, according to her testimony.

You would be surprised at just how many angels God has commissioned to work for you right now. This is why He urges us, "Let Me circumcise your heart. You cannot accomplish anything through your intellect or abilities. You need Me to perform this impossible work for you. So, turn to Me. Trust Me to do it. I have all the resources you need."

Only after the Israelites were circumcised were they ready to go to battle. They no longer had confidence in themselves or relied on their fleshly enthusiasm. As their bodies were being healed physically, their spirits were being calmed by God's Spirit. Now they were ready to listen to the Lord.

3. We Have to Experience the Passover.

The Israelites had crossed the Jordan, declaring war on their stronghold. They had been circumcised, swearing off all confidence in their flesh. Now they had to experience the Passover. "The children of Israel encamped in Gilgal, and kept the passover on the fourteenth day of the month at even in the plains of Jericho" (Joshua 5:10).

God instituted the Passover celebration in Exodus 12 as a security measure for Israel. It was meant to protect them against destruction. First, a lamb was to be slain, and its blood was to be sprinkled over their doorposts.

> And they shall take of the blood, and strike it on the two side posts and on the upper door post of the houses, where they shall eat it. . . . And the blood shall be to you for a token upon the houses where ye are: and when I see the blood, I will pass over you, and the plague shall not be upon you to destroy you, when I smite the land of Egypt.
>
> Exodus 12:7, 13

Passover was an annual observance. It was to be held during the month that Israel had come out of Egypt, and on the fourteenth day of that month. On that day, Israel's annual calendar began. It became known as the "beginning of months."

Amazingly, on the day the Israelites recovered from their circumcision at Gilgal, it was the fourteenth day of that first month. Just as they were about to do battle against the stronghold in their Promised Land, the day came to celebrate the Passover. How perfect God's timing is! I believe this passage shows us that the Lord has set a day and time for everything in our lives. It all takes place under His heavenly gaze and His divine control. I call this "Holy Ghost timing."

That evening the Israelites offered the Passover sacrifice. They built an altar and brought forth an unblemished lamb to be slain. First, the animal's blood was drained into a vessel. Then a high priest dipped hyssop into the blood and used it to sprinkle the blood over the people. Finally, the lamb's carcass was consumed by fire on the altar.

There, in the shadow of Jericho's great, high walls, God's people experienced the sprinkling of the blood of the lamb. This blood sprinkling signified that God saw His people released from the guilt of all their sins. "Without shedding of blood is no remission" (Hebrews 9:22).

I believe that Joshua preached a powerful sermon at this Passover service. What he actually said does not appear in Scripture, but I think I know the nature of the sermon he delivered. He knew this new generation had ears to hear the voice of the Lord. They had crossed the Jordan and declared war, and now they were ready to go all the way to obtain God's promises. But there was something remaining in their hearts that the Lord wanted to deal with.

Perhaps at this point Joshua reminded the people of what had happened just a short time earlier; their hearts had been fully exposed. Now he recalled to them the last words Moses had spoken to them: "I know thy rebellion, and thy stiff neck: behold while I am yet alive with you this day, ye have been rebellious against the LORD; and how much more after my death?" (Deuteronomy 31:27). The original Hebrew word for *rebellious* in this verse means "bitter, disobedient."

Joshua knew Moses was right: The people he was leading now still had serious problems. They were bent on backsliding, always falling back into unbelief. Moreover, as Joshua considered the people's sins, he had to look at the condition of his own heart as well. He knew he was as human as the other Israelites.

Knowing God by Name

At times he had no doubt been plagued with his own doubts and questions.

Now Joshua stood before the crowd with a dilemma. How could he remind the Israelites about this exposure of their hearts without making them feel condemned? They were on the brink of going into battle against the stronghold of Jericho. They could not possibly make war against that fortified enemy if they thought God was mad at them. If they harbored thoughts of condemnation in the midst of battle, they would become weak and lose heart.

Joshua knew he could not lead the people into battle this way. I believe he said something like this: "Here we stand, a people chosen and blessed by God. We are full of courage, ready to lay down our lives to gain freedom and enter into the fullness of God's promises. Yet our hearts have been fully exposed. Many still carry roots of bitterness toward the Lord. Others have been disobedient to His Word. How can we overcome the stronghold of Jericho, unless our wicked hearts are cleaned up? We cannot just cast the rebellion and bitterness out of ourselves. We do not have the power to do that."

This describes our dilemma today as well. None of us is without disobedience in some area. Our failure may be overt sin, or it may be evil thoughts that plague our minds. Both are reminiscent of our old lives in the wilderness, before we were saved, and both hold us back from entering fully into God's victory. There is only one hope for us: We must come to the blood. By the sprinkling of the blood of the lamb, the Lord will cover our sins and look upon us as purged from all iniquity. Thank God for the blood of the perfect Lamb who was slain for us!

> If the blood of bulls and of goats, and the ashes of an heifer sprinkling the unclean, sanctifieth to the purifying of the flesh: how much more shall the blood of Christ, who through the eternal Spirit offered himself without spot to God, purge your conscience from dead works to serve the living God?
>
> Hebrews 9:13–14

After the Israelites observed the Passover, they were secured by the blood of the lamb. They no longer had to carry the condemnation of their sin. The only thing that mattered now was how God viewed them. And He beheld them as pure: "He hath not beheld iniquity in Jacob, neither hath he seen perverseness in Israel: the LORD his God is with him, and the shout of a king is among them" (Numbers 23:21).

The Israelites could now enter into spiritual warfare knowing their heavenly King saw no iniquity in them. Likewise, this is the only way we can go against our Jericho strongholds—by laying our sins on the Lamb. If we do not, we are already defeated. The author of Hebrews tells us that this is why God swore an oath to bless us by delivering us from all sin: "Wherein God . . . confirmed it by an oath: that . . . we might have a strong consolation . . . which hope we have as an anchor of the soul" (Hebrews 6:17–19).

The Joshua Company was now over the Jordan—circumcised, secured by the blood and anchored in God's forgiving grace. They were brimming with confidence in the Lord, able to move forward with no condemnation. This brought them to the fourth requirement.

4. We Have to Face the Walled City of Jericho.

Every one of us has his own Jericho. I am speaking of a walled-up stronghold that hinders us from moving forward into fullness in Christ. In almost every case, this stronghold is a single besetting sin—a habit, lust or character weakness that has become entrenched in us, surrounded by impregnable walls. Your Jericho may be pride, fear of man, an out-of-control temper, a roving eye or a root of bitterness. No matter what it is, if you have not let God deal with it you can be sure it is keeping you back from the marvelous things He has prepared for you.

Knowing God by Name

We may be tempted to think, *I don't have any strongholds in my life. I'm not holding onto a besetting sin.* Yet look at the words of the apostle John: "If we say that we have no sin, we deceive ourselves, and the truth is not in us. . . . If we say that we have not sinned, we make him a liar, and his word is not in us" (1 John 1:8, 10). We all have our Jerichos, and we are terribly deceived if we sit around smugly congratulating ourselves, believing we do not have any strongholds that we need to be delivered from.

Actually, Christians generally acknowledge their Jerichos but many refuse to declare war. Instead they give up the battle, thinking, *This sin is too deep in me. Its roots are too strong, too entrenched. I can't do anything to break its hold on me. I'll just have to live with it and do the best I can. I'll have to keep asking Jesus for forgiveness, because there is nothing I can do to stop it.* There are awful consequences to coexisting with Jericho. We see this illustrated in Numbers 13–14 when the twelve Israelite spies under Moses' leadership came back from spying out the land.

These men had just visited Jericho and were awed by the city's forbidding walls. Archaeologists suggest those walls were so wide that chariot races might have been held on top of them. A woman named Rahab had a house embedded in one of Jericho's famous walls, and many other homes were built into them as well. The mere sight of the city's high, thick walls was enough to send the Israelite spies back to their camp disheartened. Scripture says that most of these men brought back an evil report to Israel: "The cities are walled, and very great. . . . We be not able to go up against the people; for they are stronger than we" (Numbers 13:28, 31).

When the Israelites heard this news they completely lost heart. They refused to go up against Jericho and its walled fortress. What were the consequences of their refusal? The Lord told them:

> Surely they shall not see the land which I sware unto their fathers, neither shall any of them that provoked me see it . . . as ye have

spoken in mine ears, so will I do to you: your carcasses shall fall in this wilderness . . . in this wilderness they shall be consumed, and there they shall die. And the men, which Moses sent to search the land, who returned and made all the congregation to murmur against him, by bringing up a slander upon the land, even those men that did bring up the evil report upon the land, died by the plague before the LORD.

Numbers 14:23, 28–29, 35–37

This is what happens to everyone who refuses to declare war on a besetting sin. If we try to coexist with a Jericho in our lives, we will bring down spiritual death on ourselves. Our faith will end up on the ash heap.

My mind immediately turns to several examples. I remember a man here at Times Square Church who always carried a briefcase with him. After years of attending our church, the man took me aside one day and whispered that he wanted to show me what was inside. He opened the briefcase and it was filled with piles of filthy pornography. He told me sadly, "I'm hopelessly addicted. I have tried for years to quit, but I can't. There is just no hope for me." Both his head and his heart had been fried by the habit he indulged in. He was almost out of his mind from constantly entertaining thoughts of horrible lust. At some point he had resigned himself to it, deciding, "It's all too much for me to handle. This wall inside me is never going to come down."

A minister once wrote me this tragic confession: "Years ago I grew bitter toward a pastor because of the abuse he heaped on me. I refused to deal with my bitterness. Instead, I told the Lord, 'Don't call me, I'll call You.' In other words, I said to God, 'If I ever get over this, I'll let You know. Just don't bother me about it now. I can't handle it.' It has now been more than twenty years since I began harboring the hurt this man caused me. In all that time God has never once spoken to me. I have to confess, the hurt I once harbored is still there." This minister, a man called to preach the Gospel of grace, has been wandering in a wilderness for over two decades. His life is plagued by deadly bitterness.

As my mind goes back over the years, I see the faces of many once-great ministers of God—powerful, mightily used preachers—who refused to declare war on their sins. They never determined to do battle against their besetting habits: adulterous affairs, addictions to pornography, bitterness, anger, dishonest financial dealings and lust for fame. Instead, they allowed their Jerichos to live on.

Finally, the Spirit of God left them. Many of these men divorced their wives and left the ministry. Some married younger women. In the process, they lost everything—their families, their ministries, their self-respect and the regard of their peers. Some settled for work at menial jobs. Some became alcoholics who died on the streets. Others died of deadly diseases within a few years. I remember once seeing a fallen evangelist—a once-godly man I had admired as a boy—hobbling around with a cane. After a lifetime of adultery, his body had been emaciated by the disease of sin. Yet, all the while, he should have been involved in God's work fulltime, ministering the Gospel in the calling he had been given!

In every case, these men were robbed of joy, peace, rest and God's favor. None of them entered into the fullness of God's promises. Instead, they were consumed in a wilderness of sin, and it all happened because they refused to deal with the stronghold of a besetting sin. God is telling everyone in His Church today who refuses to face his own personal stronghold—in no uncertain terms!—"Your Jericho has to come down."

Now we learn with Joshua how that is possible.

Military Impossibilities

As Joshua stood on a hill overlooking Jericho, he must have strategized for hours about how to bring down this formidable

---

stronghold. His mind must have been working overtime. *How is it possible to penetrate such an impossible stronghold when all you have at your disposal is an untrained army with a few swords? Do you dig under the walls? Do you try to scale them? Do you burn down the gates?*

God probably let his servant strategize until there simply was no strategy left. Eventually Joshua must have realized there was no human way to get through those walls. It was an utterly hopeless situation. He had to resign himself to the fact that it was going to take a miracle. He might have prayed, "God, unless You undertake this work, it can't be done." Then, suddenly, a man appeared before Joshua, wielding a sword. Let's look at these verses again:

> It came to pass, when Joshua was by Jericho, that he lifted up his eyes and looked, and, behold, there stood a man over against him with his sword drawn in his hand: and Joshua went unto him, and said unto him, Art thou for us, or for our adversaries? And he said, Nay; but as captain of the host of the Lord am I now come. And Joshua fell on his face to the earth, and did worship, and said unto him, What saith my lord unto his servant? And the captain of the Lord's host said unto Joshua, Loose thy shoe from off thy foot; for the place whereon thou standest is holy. And Joshua did so.

> Joshua 5:13–15

I believe, with most Bible scholars, that this captain of the Lord's host was Jesus. Joshua apparently recognized Him as being Jehovah. Otherwise he never would have bowed and worshiped Him, because he would not worship an angel.

Joshua cried out to this figure, "Are you for us, or against us?" At first glance, the captain's reply seems curt, aloof, even condescending. He avoids answering Joshua's question directly, replying instead, "I am the captain of the Lord's host." This phrase translates in Hebrew as, "I am come as *Jehovah Tsebaioth.*" He is saying, in other words, "You have asked the wrong question, Joshua. There is no side for Me to be on. This war is not between you and Jericho. It is a war between Jehovah and Satan, and I am *Jehovah Tsebaioth*, captain of the Lord's heavenly army. You need to know this is not your battle, but Mine.

"Here is the key to all victory. You have crossed the Jordan, you have been circumcised, you have been blood-secured—yet you still face an overwhelming battle. This warfare is totally beyond your strength and ability. So the Lord comes to you with a powerful assurance: You have to see that this battle is not yours, but Mine. I am committed to do all the fighting for you."

Joshua immediately understood this revelation of God's power and might. He must have been totally relieved to hand over his sword. He probably said, "Thank You, Lord. I didn't have a plan." I imagine Jesus answering, "Of course you didn't. There is no plan for man in this kind of warfare. The battle is all Mine."

The devil had infiltrated Jericho years before the Israelites arrived, making sure it was fortified by his own unseen powers. He was fully aware of God's promise to give the land to Israel. So he directed his demonic forces to dig into the city with every conceivable armament. It was a massive effort from hell to thwart the seed, to keep it from moving toward its fulfillment in the coming Messiah.

So it is with a besetting sin; Jericho becomes entrenched in you by the devil's unseen forces. This does not mean you are demon-possessed. It simply means there is one stronghold left, one hidden place in your heart where sin has dug in and refused to let go. You cannot enter into the Lord's fullness until that stronghold comes down. It simply has to be dealt with. But you have no power to do battle against it.

Only the Lord's unseen army can conquer this stronghold. On your own, you could strategize for years without ever coming up with an effective plan. You would end up thinking, *There is no way I can ever defeat this enemy. Time after time, battle after battle,*

it has proven too strong for me. I know I will only fail again if I keep
trying to go up against it. I don't even have the strength to try anymore.
I guess I'll always be at the mercy and power of this enemy.

No, never! The Lord is telling you, "I am going to fight this battle for you. I have the power to dig out those demon powers. You have already done all you need to do. You have crossed your Jordan, you have been circumcised and you have been blood-secured. Now you need only to move forward at My word. Soon you will see Me bring down this stronghold before your eyes."

This is just what Christ was communicating to Joshua when He appeared to him. He was saying, "Joshua, the enemy has fortified Jericho with unseen principalities and powers of darkness. It is going to take an unseen host from glory to cast him down. So I come to you now as *Jehovah Tsebaioth*—captain of the Lord of hosts. I have at My command a huge, mighty army with troops, chariots and horses you know nothing about. This is not your battle—it is the Lord's. The host of heavenly beings who act on My command are going to tear these walls down. They are going to wipe out Jericho from the face of the earth forever. Your job in this battle is just to keep moving on. Simply walk in obedience to My word. My unseen host will deal with bringing down this stronghold."

Many Christians today become overwhelmed as they try to confront their strongholds. When they see their Jerichos towering before them, they panic. As they contemplate doing battle against this enemy, they begin to wither. Soon the enemy has beaten them back into the wilderness. He has convinced them they have to remain helpless until they die. Then *Jehovah Tsebaioth* appears to them with these words of reassurance: "You do not have to fear this enemy. Just come under the blood. I will cover you with all manner of divine protection. Keep walking and talking with Me. All the while I will be doing battle for you. I have a whole host at My disposal to do war against your Jericho.

You have to know that the forces of *Jehovah Tsebaioth* are always at work on your behalf."

As Israel kept moving toward Jericho, a whirlwind of activity took place in the unseen world. Princes of glory did combat with the principalities of hell. Each day, as the Israelites marched around Jericho, heavenly forces were at work undermining the city's walls. God's hosts loosened every brick and weakened the foundations.

What do you imagine the Israelites thought as they marched daily around Jericho's walls? I believe they probably had doubts about the battle. After all, during the whole week they marched, they never saw any evidence that God was at work. They simply did their marching every day and went back to camp at night. Not once during that week did they see any visible results of a heavenly host's work on their behalf.

Then the seventh day came. In obedience to God's command, the Israelites blew their trumpets—and Jericho's mighty walls came tumbling down. Can you imagine the thunderous crash as the enemy's centuries-old stronghold was brought to nothing? Yet it was not the Israelites' shouting that brought down those walls. It was the host of Jehovah pushing them down with supernatural might.

Bringing Down the Walls

What about the enemy's stronghold in your life? Have you lived for years with a habitual sin you despise, never gaining victory over it? As you face it now, are you at a loss about what to do? It is time to declare war on your Jericho. Give up all hope of ever overcoming it by your own strength and willpower. Instead, bow down to the power of the Holy Ghost. Hand your sword over to God and trust in His covenant promise to defeat all your enemies. You will discover *Jehovah Tsebaioth,* the Lord of hosts. You will see Him go to work for you.

Your role is simply to keep moving forward in faith and obedience. Do not faint or allow yourself to despair. Just be faithful to keep walking on with Jesus. He is the captain of the Lord's hosts and He is faithful to take down your stronghold. He gave Israel specific directions for battle and He will give you directions for your path as well. You can trust Him to direct His hosts of angels to do His bidding on your behalf.

We can get discouraged in our battle against Jericho if we do not see results right away. We may think, *I am moving forward in obedience, just as the Lord directed me. I am trusting Him with all my heart and I am not fearful anymore. But, this stronghold is still in me. I don't see it budging at all. Is the Lord working for me or not? Where are the results?*

We have to remember Israel's example at Jericho. Those lovers of God could not see the battle going on in the heavenlies. But in the unseen world, God's army was winning victory after victory. On the seventh day, that great host cried, "Let us finish the work." They pushed down the walls, crushing all of Jericho's resistance. They put every evil defender to flight.

Likewise, you may not see immediate results. Yet while you are walking with Jesus—moving forward in faith, fully persuaded that you are secured by the blood—your Lord's hosts are waging war for you. They are doing battle against the demonic principality that has entrenched itself as a stronghold in your life. You can rest assured, your Jericho is coming down. *Jehovah Tsebaioth,* the Lord of hosts, is at work for you. So just keep walking, keep moving on. Your day of total victory is soon to come.

five

Jehovah Shalom

The Lord Our Peace

Knowing (and believing in) God's character as revealed in His names provides great protection against enemy attack. God declared through Hosea, "My people are destroyed for lack of knowledge" (Hosea 4:6). The implication here is powerful. God is telling us that having an intimate knowledge of His nature and character, as revealed through His names, is a powerful shield against Satan's lies.

This brings us to another of our Lord's names: *Jehovah Shalom.* We find this name mentioned in the book of Judges. Here, the Lord revealed Himself to Gideon in the form of an angel:

When Gideon perceived that he was an angel of the LORD, Gideon said, Alas, O LORD God! For because I have seen an angel of the LORD face to face. And the LORD said unto him, Peace be unto thee; fear not: thou shalt not die. Then Gideon built an altar there unto the LORD, and called it Jehovah-shalom.

Judges 6:22–24

What does this name, *Jehovah Shalom,* mean exactly? I could digress here into an extended discussion of the meanings of this well-known Hebrew word, *shalom.* Suffice it to say, *shalom* is one of the most meaningful expressions in the Hebrew language. To this day, the word is held dear in the hearts of Jews everywhere. Even as a Christian, you have probably heard the warm greeting "Shalom." Perhaps you have used it on occasion, lifting your hand in greeting to your brothers and sisters in Christ, saying, "Shalom! The peace of God be with you." You have probably learned that this Jewish expression has something to do with having peace.

As a noun, the Hebrew word *shalom* means "completeness, health and welfare." It implies being whole, in harmony with God and man, having wholesome relationships. It also indicates a state of being at ease—not restless, having peace both inwardly and outwardly, being at rest both spiritually and emotionally. In short, *shalom* signifies wholeness in a life or work. As a verb, *shalom* means to be completed or finished, or to make peace.

I have read several scholarly works concerning the definitions of *shalom.* In my studies, I have discovered that the word's multiple meanings are wonderfully varied and deep. This is especially true of *shalom* as it relates to Jesus Christ, the Prince of peace, who provides His people with supernatural peace in every dimension of life. Yet once more I am driven to ask, "What does this particular name of God have to do with me and with the church today? What is the Lord trying to say to His people through this name, *Jehovah Shalom?*"

Knowing God by Name

Every time God revealed a characteristic of His nature to someone, that person was in a time of crisis, as we have seen. The revelation always came when God's servant needed a fresh vision of the Lord to see him through. Each time, God brought forth a specific aspect of His nature to instill in His servant the faith needed to accomplish His eternal purpose.

The revelation of *Jehovah Shalom* was given to one such man in crisis—Gideon. As we explore this passage in full, we will see that the only way Gideon could have received such a revelation was through the Holy Ghost—and it changed Gideon's life.

An Angelic Visitation

In His great mercy, the Lord sent a warning to Israel. Out of nowhere an angel appeared to God's people at Bochim, delivering an awesome rebuke.

> An angel of the LORD came up from Gilgal to Bochim, and said, I made you to go up out of Egypt, and have brought you unto the land which I sware unto your fathers; and I said, I will never break my covenant with you. And ye shall make no league with the inhabitants of this land; ye shall throw down their altars: but ye have not obeyed my voice: why have ye done this? Wherefore I also said, I will not drive them out from before you; but they shall be as thorns in your sides, and their gods shall be a snare unto you.
>
> Judges 2:1–3

This was a stern warning to a compromised nation, yet I believe it was also meant for every generation to come, including the church today, upon whom the ends of the world have come. The Lord is giving us the same kind of warning:

"I brought you up out of the bondage of sin. I delivered you and set you free from everything that bound you. Then, in My love for you, I brought you into a place of mercy and blessing. What did

I ask of you in return? I commanded you to separate yourselves from the things of this world. I told you to flee its evil—to avoid getting entangled in its pleasures, to forsake everything having to do with its idolatry. Nothing of flesh or sin could remain in your life. You were to rid yourselves completely of everything that would rob you of power to stand before your enemy.

"Then I gave you a promise. I said if you would obey Me in this one matter—if you refused to spare a single wicked way, desiring a pure heart—I would supply you with all the power you needed to remain free. I would send My Spirit to empower you. Through His strength, you would be able to utterly mortify every hindrance in your life. Nothing could keep you from being brought into My fullness.

"For years now, I have lovingly warned you to forsake your sinful desires. I have laid out My word clearly before you, in gentleness and kindness. I have sent messenger after messenger to remind you that you cannot coexist with your sin or allow any compromise. Yet you persist in clinging to your idols. Why do you continue to disobey Me? How can you not see the danger you are in? How can you keep coddling your idol, when it has served only to deepen your greed, materialism and depression? You thought you could contain your lusts, keep them on a leash, but now they have led you straight into the enemy's hands."

When the Israelites heard this reproving word, they were convicted to the point of tears. The Bible tells us, "It came to pass, when the angel of the LORD spake these words unto all the children of Israel, that the people lifted up their voice, and wept. And they called the name of that place Bochim" (Judges 2:4–5). The name *Bochim* means "a place of weeping and wailing."

I believe the Israelites' tears were real. The people felt awful about their sin, and they expressed their anguish openly. Yet, sadly, their conviction was short-lived. Scripture says they still did not let go of their idols. They may have been good weepers, but none of them brought his idols to the altar to be destroyed.

They thought they could go forth in service to the Lord while clutching their filthy idols.

Here is another important lesson for us today: In itself, conviction of sin cannot deliver anyone from bondage. Let's say your sin is exposed publicly. It brings you sadness, sorrow and humiliation. It may even cause you to weep mightily. But this does not mean that you have been healed of your sin. The truth is, weeping and wailing often accompany a shallow, halfhearted repentance. The real fruit of genuine repentance is not just tears of grief, but a willingness to forsake the sin that led to such sorrow.

I have personally witnessed the so-called open confessions of many ministers and church leaders who were caught in sin. When their sins were exposed—bondages such as adultery, alcoholism and pornography—these men were overcome with emotion. They cried out publicly, "Yes, I have sinned." Great tears poured down their cheeks, and they voiced pitiful cries of anguish.

Suddenly the people surrounding these men set aside their shock, hurt and anger. They were moved to compassion for their ministers. So they gathered around them, offering comfort, support and pledges of restoration. That is the Christ-like thing to do.

Yet within a short period of time, the supposedly repentant ministers went back to their sins. Their repentance was shallow, halfhearted and ultimately self-serving. This has taught me an important lesson over the years: *It is not enough merely to weep over your sins.*

That is the exact message Malachi gave to a nation of adulterous Israelite men. The prophet cried out, "This have ye done again, covering the altar of the LORD with tears, with weeping, and with crying out, insomuch that he [God] regardeth not the offering" (Malachi 2:13). Malachi was saying, in essence, "You come to the altar weeping big tears, ready to offer a great sacrifice. But God sees the way you're still deceiving your wife. On the outside you are repentant, grieving, sorrowful. But inside you continue your treachery. You refuse to let go of your adulterous relationship."

The book of Judges is one of the saddest, most tragic chapters in the history of God's people. Consider the final summary verse of this Old Testament book: "In those days there was no king in Israel: every man did that which was right in his own eyes" (Judges 21:25). That is where it all ended—with each of God's people doing what he thought was right for himself. Everyone was able to give an excuse for his own sin and evil behavior. Few were deeply convicted by God's Word.

Yet the book of Judges is more than the tragic history of the backsliding nation of Israel. It is also the story of our times, reflecting a church filled with believers who refuse to forsake their secret sins.

Are We Losing the Race Against Apathy?

I see something taking place in the Church all over the world today that grieves God's heart: a widespread apathy toward sin. God's people are no longer outraged about the filth and evil bombarding their lives and homes. On the contrary, millions of believers sit by passively and let their minds become saturated with sensual movies, videos, television, the Internet, magazines and other media. It is unbelievable how these Christians willingly allow their lusts to be fed as their imaginations are filled with deep roots of evil.

If you think I am focusing too much on the secret sins of Christians, then I say you are out of touch with what is happening in the world today. You must know nothing of how widespread the infection of sin is among God's people. I cite to you, for example, the scores of Christians who flock to movie theaters each week and hear the name of Christ used as a curse word. I have never understood how anyone who fears almighty God and wishes to walk righteously before Him can sit by idly as the Lord's name is being damned. That is simply beyond my comprehension. Yet multitudes of believers are doing just that. Little by little, they are drifting deeper into pits of secret, hidden sin. Slowly but surely, their sense of conviction is being drained out of them. They do not realize it, but their minds are being corrupted by what they are allowing their eyes to feast on.

In His great mercy, God is always faithful to send prophets to warn His people. Today the Lord is sending us His holy watchmen—preachers, teachers, evangelists—with warnings to heed His Word: "You must utterly destroy your besetting sin. You simply can't allow any evil way to remain in you. You have to declare war on the lusts and seductions of this age."

The Bible warns that if we continue to hold onto our secret sins, we will eventually forsake God and be given over to our lusts. Our Lord may deal with us patiently month after month, year after year. He may send us compassionate warnings through His faithful messengers. But, ultimately, if we refuse to heed His Word, we will drift away from Him completely. We will finally become a helpless prey before our enemy.

This is just what happened to Israel. The Bible tells us,

> They forsook the LORD God of their fathers . . . and followed other gods . . . and provoked the LORD to anger . . . and he delivered them into the hands of spoilers that spoiled them, and he sold them into the hands of their enemies round about, so that they could not any longer stand before their enemies. . . . The hand of the LORD was against them for evil . . . and they were greatly distressed.
>
> Judges 2:12–15

Time after time, it was the same old story. The Israelites always promised to obey, but their words had no substance. They were never able totally to overcome their enemies or enjoy a lasting victory. Try to imagine the scores of Israelites who were lost during those long periods of sin and backsliding. If they had only embraced God's Word when they heard it, they would have had the strength to withstand the hostile attacks of their enemies. Instead they never allowed the preaching and teaching they heard to penetrate their hearts. They never allowed the true fear of God to take root. They ended up being easy prey for their enemies.

For seven years, Israel paid a terrible price for her sins. Judges 6 describes an awful scenario in Israel:

> The children of Israel did evil in the sight of the LORD: and the LORD delivered them into the hand of Midian seven years. And the hand of Midian prevailed against Israel: and because of the Midianites the children of Israel made them the dens which are in the mountains, and caves, and strongholds. And so it was, when Israel had sown, that the Midianites came up, and the Amalekites, and the children of the east, even they came up against them; and they encamped against them, and destroyed the increase of the earth . . . and left no sustenance for Israel, neither sheep, nor ox, nor ass.
>
> For they came up with their cattle and their tents, and they came as grasshoppers for multitude; for both they and their camels were without number: and they entered into the land to destroy it. And Israel was greatly impoverished because of the Midianites; and the children of Israel cried unto the Lord.
>
> Judges 6:1–6

Disobedience Brings Discipline

At harvest time every year, Israel was invaded by the Midianites. These enemies knew exactly when Israel's fields and vineyards became ripe and when the cattle gave birth. For seven straight years they migrated to Israel's borders on their camels, camped just beyond the outskirts and waited. Then, when the time was right, they swooped down on Israel like locusts. They descended on the fields, taking everything in sight—fruit, crops, cattle. They literally wiped out the harvest, leaving God's people impoverished: "They . . . destroyed the increase of the earth . . . and left no sustenance for Israel" (6:4).

The Israelites could not understand why they were so harassed year after year. How could God allow their enemies to plunder them? After all, they had enjoyed forty years of prosperity under the prophetess Deborah. Why could they not stand up to the Midianites now and thwart these enemies' attacks? What had brought Israel to such a shameful level of cowardice? Wasn't God on their side, working on their behalf? If He was, why did they have to live in continual fear and poverty?

For years they had to hide in caves for protection. They held prayer meetings in those caves, crying out to God, "Lord, we haven't forsaken You. You see us calling on You day after day, weeping and interceding. Please tell us why this is happening. Why do we have to endure so much trouble from our enemies? Why don't we enjoy Your peace anymore, as we did under Your servant Deborah? Why don't we see You working on our behalf?"

Let me point out here that not all trouble is a result of sin. As the psalmist writes, "Many are the afflictions of the righteous" (Psalm 34:19). But note the second half of this verse: "But the LORD delivereth him out of them all." According to God's Word, our Lord, in His time, delivers His righteous servants out of their afflictions. They do not have to live in a constant state of distress. They enjoy peace in their times of trial. They may undergo seasons of affliction, but the Lord is forever present to reassure them and deliver them. Eventually, night turns to day.

This was not the case with Israel. Why did the people have to endure constant distress? It was because of their continual idolatry. They acted holy before God, offering up prayers of weeping and intercession. But as soon as their prayer meetings ended, they sneaked off to kneel before their altars of Baal. In fact, throughout those seven years of raids from the Midianites, Gideon's father, Joash, kept an altar to Baal in his backyard. Why would any Israelite do such a thing? He did so because, like the other Israelites, he was jealous of the prosperity the Midianites enjoyed. The Israelites reasoned, "Our enemies are prospering. They have our fruit and provisions. Their god provides them with everything while we sit here starving. Those Midianites must have one powerful god. Obviously, we can't afford to offend him." So the Lord's people became hypocrites, two-faced worshipers. They gave lip service to Jehovah while paying tribute to another god.

At the very height of Israel's poverty, God sent another prophet to expose His people's sin. He wanted to show them exactly why they were distressed and impoverished. Scripture describes the scene this way:

> It came to pass, when the children of Israel cried unto the LORD because of the Midianites, that the LORD sent a prophet unto the children of Israel, which said unto them, Thus saith the LORD God of Israel, I brought you up from Egypt, and brought you forth out of the house of bondage; and I delivered you out of the hand of the Egyptians, and out of the hand of all that oppressed you, and drove them out from before you, and gave you their land; and I said unto you, I am the LORD your God; fear not the gods of the Amorites, in whose land ye dwell: but ye have not obeyed my voice.
>
> Judges 6:7–10

God Speaks Through Jesus

Who was the unnamed prophet who delivered this word? Scripture makes it clear: This stranger was the Lord Himself (a Christophany). Often in the Old Testament, Christ is called "the angel of the Lord." Later in this same passage, we see the stranger referred to that way: "There came an angel of the LORD . . . and the angel of the LORD appeared to him [Gideon]" (Judges 6: 11–12). Then, just a few verses down, we see this angelic figure referred to as the Lord: "The LORD said unto him [Gideon], Peace be unto thee; fear not" (verse 23).

When the unnamed prophet appeared on the scene, Gideon and his family were among the poorest of Israel's poor. They were living off the handfuls of grain Gideon brought home from a hidden threshing floor. Gideon was trying to eke out a living by scavenging any leftover wheat he could find. Now, as the angel of the Lord appeared, He said to Gideon: "The LORD is with thee, thou mighty man of valour" (verse 12).

On the surface these words may seem puzzling. God was speaking to a man who, like every other Israelite, had sat by and done nothing for seven years. Indeed, in all the years the Midianites attacked Israel, Gideon had displayed not one bit of evidence of valor. He had not even protested his father's pagan altar. Like everyone else, Gideon had lived in fear and bondage.

Yet now the Lord was instructing this man, "Go in this thy might, and thou shalt save Israel from the hand of the Midianites: have not I sent thee?" (verse 14). What might was the Lord talking about here? Where in this story do we read of any infusion of strength or power into Gideon? Did something supernatural happen during this exchange so that Gideon's doubt and fear were transformed into might? Or was he supposed to claim some divine vigor by faith?

I believe that something happened to Gideon during this scene. Scripture indicates that there was a definite transfer of power into him, an infusion of might from the Holy Ghost. We find a clue to this divine infusion in verse 14, which begins, "The LORD looked upon him." The Hebrew verb for *looked* in this verse is the same verb used in Genesis 32:30 when Jacob wrestled with the Lord. That verse reads, "Jacob called the name of the place Peniel: for I have seen God face to face, and my life is preserved." Jacob was saying, in essence, "God looked me right in the face."

What was the outcome of Jacob's face-to-face encounter with the Lord? Scripture tells us, "As a prince hast thou power with

God and with men, and hast prevailed" (Genesis 32:28). Evidently, a transfer of power took place when Jesus looked Jacob in the eye. With this single gesture from the Lord, Jacob received an infusion of supernatural strength that prepared him to face any foe. The apostle Paul describes this kind of supernatural transfer in New Testament terms: "We all, with open face beholding as in a glass the glory of the Lord, are changed into the same image from glory to glory" (2 Corinthians 3:18).

The book of Judges is telling us that Gideon had direct communion with God through this kind of face-to-face encounter. You might ask, "How could this be? Doesn't the Bible say it's impossible for any human being to see God and live?" You are absolutely right. The apostle John writes, "No man hath seen God at any time" (1 John 4:12). Paul concurs, writing, "The blessed and only Potentate, the King of kings, and Lord of lords; who only hath immortality, dwelling in the light which no man can approach unto; whom no man hath seen, nor can see" (1 Timothy 6:15–16).

But John qualifies his statement with this verse: "No man hath seen God at any time; [but] the only begotten Son, which is in the bosom of the Father, he hath declared him" (John 1:18). In other words, "Jesus has manifested the Father to us. We see the essence of the Father when we look at Christ, the Son."

John writes elsewhere, "The Word was made flesh, and dwelt among us, (and we beheld his glory, the glory as of the only begotten of the Father,) full of grace and truth" (John 1:14). He adds that, long before Jesus' birth, Christ "was in the world, and the world was made by him, and the world knew him not" (verse 10).

Scripture makes it clear: Over the centuries, people stood face to face with the mediator, Jesus Christ, and were changed by the experience. Jacob saw Him at Peniel, Moses on the mountaintop and Daniel in the pagan land of Babylon. Here in Judges, as Gideon communed with the Lord face to face, he also was infused with a transforming power. It was a power that would provide Israel with deliverance. The Israelites had not obtained the Promised Land through any innate power, authority or ability of their own. They had received everything through their face-to-face encounters with the Lord. Every blessing had come to them not by power, nor by might, but by the glory of God's countenance. "For they [Israel] got not the land in possession by their own sword, neither did their own arm save them: but by thy right hand, and thine arm, and the light of thy countenance, because thou hadst a favour unto them" (Psalm 44:3).

Recognizing God as Our Source

This supernatural transfer of power totally transformed Gideon. In the blink of an eye, he turned from a coward into a mighty warrior. Yet, amazingly, Gideon still had no idea he was dealing with the Lord. This passage implies that he treated Christ almost as casually as he would treat any other human being. In fact, Gideon asked the stranger to prove He was from the Lord. He demanded, "If now I have found grace in thy sight, then shew me a sign that thou talkest with me" (Judges 6:17). Can you imagine such audacity? It is as if Gideon were saying to Jesus, "If You have truly been sent from God, then do something that convinces me You are actually who You say You are."

Gideon also tried to strike a sort of deal with the Lord. He said to Him, "I'd like you to sit down and share a meal with me. So, I'm going into the kitchen now to prepare the food. Please, do me a favor and wait here until I bring it out" (see verses 17–18). What Gideon did here is unfathomable to me. He actually put God on hold! Yet the Lord responded with grace, saying, "I will tarry until thou come again" (verse 18).

After a while Gideon returned with the food—a lamb, unleavened bread and broth. Yet before he could set the meal on the table, the Lord instructed him to place the food on a nearby stone.

Then He directed Gideon to pour the broth over it all. Gideon did as he was told, and the Lord promptly lifted His staff and touched the food with it. Suddenly fire shot out of the rock and consumed the entire meal. Then, in an instant, the Lord disappeared as quickly as He had come. (He might even have vanished in the flame, as He later did before Samson's father, Manoah: "It came to pass, when the flame went up toward heaven from off the altar, that the angel of the LORD ascended in the flame of the altar" [Judges 13:20].)

Gideon was flabbergasted. The Bible says, "When Gideon perceived that he was an angel of the LORD, Gideon said, Alas, O Lord GOD! For because I have seen an angel of the LORD face to face" (Judges 6:22). Why was Gideon so shaken? He realized what God's Word said: "There shall no man see me, and live" (Exodus 33:20). Suddenly, the truth exploded in Gideon's soul. He realized, "Oh, no—this was God almighty I just encountered, and I dealt with Him casually the whole time. I treated Him as if He were a mortal, just like me."

Gideon knew this was serious business. That is why he exclaimed, "Alas, O Lord GOD." The word *alas* here is an exclamation of sorrow, regret and grief, with an apprehension of danger. Think of what must have gone through Gideon's mind: *I have been toying with the creator of the universe. I didn't respond to Him as holy, almighty God. Instead I tested Him, putting Him on trial, accusing Him of forsaking His chosen people. I even had the gall to ask Him for a sign to prove He wasn't a fake. Woe is me—I'm as good as dead!*

Sadly, Gideon's casual attitude toward almighty God can often be found in churches today. Too often Christians conceive of the Lord as someone just like themselves: a buddy, a friend, someone to go have a good time with. Don't mistake my meaning here; godly people often use endearing terms such as *Daddy* to describe the Lord. But too many believers have made God out to be a sugar daddy—a doting figure. They conceive of Him as someone who merely lectures them when they sin, suggesting, "Try to do better next time."

This image of God is one reason why there is such widespread permissiveness in the church today. Casual Christians have no vision of a holy God so they have no motivation for destroying their sinful habits. Instead, they end up coexisting with their sin, coddling their lusts. This leads directly to the kind of tragic end Judges describes: Everyone does what is right in his own eyes.

When the Lord's true identity became clear to Gideon, his eyes were opened to truth. He remembered the message of the unnamed prophet and suddenly he was filled with the righteous fear of God. Gideon acknowledged, "It's true—our own sin and disobedience have brought down all this distress on us. The Lord never left us, as we have accused Him of doing. On the contrary, we have ignored him and forsaken His ways. We have taken Him for granted, making Him into a mere mortal, like ourselves. That is why we have become an easy prey for our enemies. We have brought all this distress upon ourselves, because of our disobedience and idolatry.

"I know our holy Lord smites entire nations for disobeying His Word. How can I now disobey His call to go against Baal's army? The Lord means what He says, and if He has declared that I have might, then I'm going to believe Him. He also said He would go with me, and I know His covenant promises cannot fail. So, I will gladly go."

Please note here: Gideon did not have the peace to go forward until he acknowledged that he was dealing with a righteous, holy God. The revelation of *Jehovah Shalom*—the Lord, our peace—was given to Gideon only after he cried, "Alas, O Lord GOD." He was confessing, "Oh, Lord, I regret, grieve, sorrow and repent that I did not acknowledge You as almighty God." Then, in the exact moment Gideon recognized and honored the God he was dealing with, the Lord revealed Himself as *Jehovah*

Shalom. "The LORD said unto him, Peace be unto thee; fear not: thou shalt not die" (Judges 6:23).

God was saying to Gideon, "I am *Jehovah Shalom*—the Lord, your peace." At that point, Scripture says, "Gideon built an altar there unto the LORD, and called it Jehovah-shalom" (verse 24). Thus we come to another lesson I believe the Lord wants to teach us through this story.

Receiving *Shalom*—God's Peace—As a Gift from the Lord

Shalom cannot be earned. Nor is it given to everyone who claims to be a Christian. Multitudes of regular churchgoers do not have *shalom.* Like the people of Israel, many believers have experienced only short seasons of peace between their lengthy periods of distress. They often quote the words of the Lord: "Peace I leave with you, my peace I give unto you: not as the world giveth, give I unto you. Let not your heart be troubled, neither let it be afraid" (John 14:27). "Now the Lord of peace himself give you peace always by all means" (2 Thessalonians 3: 16). Yet, as the book of Judges shows, it is impossible to receive the Lord's *shalom* until we deal with God according to His various attributes.

How can we honor the Lord as God Most High unless we deal with Him as He really is? We know He is omnipresent, everywhere at once. He is omniscient, all knowing. He is also omnipotent, all powerful. Moreover, He is merciful, kind, patient, long-suffering, compassionate, full of love and grace. He is all of these things—yet He is much more. God is also holy, just, pure, severe, unchangeable, a despiser of sin and no respecter of persons. The apostle Paul writes soberly of these latter attributes: "Behold therefore the goodness and severity of God: on them which fell, severity; but toward thee, goodness, if thou continue in his goodness: otherwise thou also shalt be cut off" (Romans 11:22).

I believe that many Christians in this current generation have no revelation of the almighty God with whom we have to deal. They do not know the God of Acts, who slew two members of a Spirit-filled church because they lied to the Holy Ghost. They have ignored the God who refuses to forgive those who do not forgive others. They do not believe in the God who said that He will judge mercilessly all who refuse to show mercy to their brothers. Here is a God, Paul says, whose wrath "is revealed from heaven against all ungodliness and unrighteousness of men, who hold the truth in unrighteousness" (Romans 1:18).

As I look back over my life, I recall many times of distress, trouble and restlessness. I see now that, during such times, I had no power to stand against the enemy as I should have. I now understand why I lacked God's peace for a time, even though I had a genuine love for the Lord. The fact is, I did not see the Lord as a holy God. I ignored all the Scriptures about His wrath and justice. Instead, I focused only on those passages having to do with His love and mercy. I was unknowingly rejecting God in favor of what I thought He *should* be like.

I also see that, in those times of distress, the Lord was urging me to deal with certain strongholds in my life, such as my temper. But I was not willing to face those things. I did not want to deal with them righteously. Now, like Gideon, I look back on those times and cry out, "Oh, Lord—I took You for granted. If only I had known who You were. If only I had understood Your holiness, Your justice, Your righteousness and Your wrath against sin!"

How do we dare to continue sinning so casually in God's presence? How dare we sit in His house singing, praising and appearing to be righteous, when all along we are gossiping, slandering our brothers and sisters— committing gross sins? How do we dare to live double lives, unafraid of God's wrath and discipline? How dare we seek justification for all our evil actions? If only we knew whom we were dealing with, we would cry out as Gideon did, "Alas, my Lord and my God. Woe is me—I am sinning before the holy, righteous judge of all men."

We will never receive the Lord's *shalom* until we realize, "This is serious business! This is God almighty I am dealing with, creator and sustainer of the universe. I cannot continue taking Him for granted—I cannot live with my sin as if He is deaf and blind. I had better recognize that I am indulging all these habits before a righteous judge who means what He says about His holiness!

"Oh, Lord, I'm grieved by my sin. I realize I have tried to serve You while still holding onto my idol. I have treated You as if You were someone weak, like me. I have doubted what You have said to me in Your Word. I have questioned Your love and leading. Please, Father, forgive me. Open my eyes and reveal Your Holy Godhood to me."

Jehovah Shalom—A Gideon Revelation

Do you tremble at God's Word? Are you ready to obey everything it says? If so, you will receive the revelation of *Jehovah Shalom*. He will come to you personally as "the Lord, your peace," filling your spirit with supernatural strength against every enemy. You cannot earn this kind of peace; it is a gift from God. Nor can you work it up. It comes to you only when you recognize and honor the One you live before: almighty God, holy and righteous.

When Gideon received the revelation of *Jehovah Shalom,* he must have been comforted by this thought: "He is truly God almighty—high, holy and righteous, but He just came to me in mercy! Didn't He approach me in pure love? Yes, He is holy—but this holy God made the first move toward me. He took the initiative. He came to me in my doubt, laziness and disobedience. He had every right to cast me aside. But He offered me power, might and clear direction instead. The Lord came to deliver me, not to damn me."

         Knowing God by Name

That is what Christianity is all about. Jesus came to you in your sin, and that ought to bring hope, joy and peace to your heart. He had every right to cast you aside. But He came to you speaking deliverance, empowerment, courage and valor instead.

Make no mistake: The Lord did not choose Gideon because He saw something great in him. No, it was as a gift that He revealed Himself to Gideon as *Jehovah Shalom*. Today the Lord makes this same offer to us. He is telling us, just as He told Gideon: "I am about to send you forth to do battle against your enemy. Don't worry—I am going to send you out with My peace filling your heart."

Our response should be like Gideon's: "The Lord says I am a person of courage and valor, and I know He is a holy God who cannot lie. So no matter how I feel—regardless of discouragement or past sin—I am going to trust what my Lord has said to me. He has commanded me to go, so I will go."

Now you can go forward with *Jehovah Shalom*—the Lord, your peace—because He has given Himself to you.

six

Jehovah Tsidkenu

The Lord Our Righteousness

Most Christians today share the same concept of righteousness. As we understand it, being righteous means having a combination of the following traits: uprightness, morality, virtuousness, good conduct, avoidance of evil and of fleshly temptations.

We all know believers who embody these wonderful traits. They are faithful to the Lord's work and to fellowshipping with His people. They are faithful to their spouses. They don't smoke, drink, curse or carouse. They don't cut corners on their jobs or cheat on their taxes. They don't defile their hearts with filthy videos, movies or TV.

These people are kind, considerate, gentle and soft-spoken. They never gossip or speak against others. Instead, they say only good things about people, including those who wrong them. In short, they walk a good, straight path of faith. As we consider their example, we cannot help but think, "There goes a righteous man. There goes a righteous woman."

There is a fundamental problem with thinking of righteousness in this way. You see, you can possess all of these wonderful qualities—you can do every good thing and look upright in every way—and still be unrighteous in God's eyes. All of these traits can be the result of pride and the kind of hard work that focuses on self. Indeed, it is possible for us to arrive at this kind of moral life through a fierce struggle with our flesh. We can attain all the human graces and still fall infinitely short of righteousness in God's eyes.

I have met many non-Christians, for example, who are very good people. They are meek, kind and loving. They will do virtually anything to help anyone, yet they are not righteous at all, by God's definition. Sadly, the same is true of many believers. They are dedicated servants who pray diligently, read their Bibles often, give their entire lives to ministering to the poor and the needy—but they know little of being righteous by biblical standards.

I grew up in a branch of the Pentecostal church that emphasized a legalistic approach to being righteous. This brand of Pentecostalism involved struggling and sweating to obtain holiness. In recent years, God has opened my eyes to the depths of truth in the New Covenant. Today I grow sad as I recall the hardships that many Pentecostal people put themselves through over the years. Some believed, for instance, that the only way they could be righteous was to fast for forty days and nights, even though very few people could actually do this. Many ended up cheating their way through an intended fast, their consciences condemning them the whole time. They ended up being hypo-critical because they were desperate to keep up an appearance of righteousness.

Chances are good that many people who read this book will have fought valiantly to rid themselves of sinful habits. They will have struggled for years to crush the dominion of sin in their lives. You see, I have known this struggle myself. I know what it is like to want more than anything else to be an overcomer (see Revelation 2:7, 11, 17, 26; 3:5, 12, 21; 21:7), and yet to fall far short with every attempt.

I know the awful struggle of trying to break free from a strong-hold, of hating a particular sin that refuses to let go. I know the guilt, the tears, the self-hatred in being defeated over and over by that sin. I also know the endless cycle of confessing my sin, making promises to God, striving to do better and sweating it out one more time. Just at the point I thought I had made it—that I had overcome my sin and achieved a measure of holiness—I fell back into a temptation that broke my heart all over again.

Each time, I ended up going to my prayer closet and weeping before the Lord. I got so frustrated, I even yelled at God: "What do You want from me, Lord? How can I ever reach a place in my life that is pleasing to You? You know I only want to be righteous. I've tried everything—yet I fail at every turn. Why can't I ever attain righteousness?"

I did not have a true understanding of righteousness. In my opinion, very few people do. They miss the import of this Scripture:

Behold, the days come, saith the LORD, that I will raise unto David a righteous Branch, and a King shall reign and prosper, and shall execute judgment and justice in the earth. In his days Judah shall be saved, and Israel shall dwell safely: and this is his name whereby he shall be called, THE LORD OUR RIGHTEOUSNESS.

Jeremiah 23:5–6

Knowing God by Name

Understanding *Jehovah Tsidkenu*—the Lord our righteousness—is absolutely crucial to the Church's survival in these last days.

The Breastplate of Righteousness

Lately, my soul has been so gripped by what I see coming on the earth, I can hardly find words to express it. Christians are going to need the very righteousness of God Himself to make it through. I believe we are going to see an apostasy such as the Church has never known—a falling away more widespread than anything we could imagine. Hell is going to spill over its borders with unspeakable evils. The world will be besieged by lusts and temptations so seductive and powerful that untold multitudes of Christians will be overcome. Pleasure-madness will engulf our children. I believe that, before the world ends, we will see a moral collapse so overwhelming that it would cause us to faint if it were described to us today.

In 1974 I wrote a prophetic book called *The Vision.* In it, I described the beginnings of this overwhelming flood of sin. Already we are seeing many of those prophecies come to pass. I devoted an entire chapter to the phenomenon of video pornography, in which people would be able to pipe X-rated movies into their homes. I wrote this long before the advent of VCRs or cable TV, and readers at the time were shocked at the idea; they thought it could never happen. Yet today, people are not only able to bring X-rated videos into their homes, but they are able to see nudity broadcast on television every night.

The Internet is yet another purveyor of pornography into the home. Teenagers and even young children are able to pipe porn into their own bedrooms through their computers. Granted, the vast majority of *information* on the Internet is good, but 90 percent of *user activity* on the Internet involves pornography.

If the Church is going to survive the coming moral landslide, we are going to need a proper revelation of righteousness from

God's point of view. We are going to have to know how to obtain His righteousness. If we do not grasp this revelation of *Jehovah Tsidkenu*—if we do not understand the Lord our righteousness—we are going to be swept away with the rest of the world.

God gave the prophet Jeremiah a revelation of *Jehovah Tsidkenu* during a time of crisis similar to the one we face today. Jeremiah lived during the reign of King Josiah. You may recall that Josiah was a righteous king, a man who walked humbly before the Lord. You may also remember that one hundred years before Josiah's ascension to the throne of Judah, the sister nation of Israel had been dispersed and taken captive. During that period, God had hoped Judah would learn from Israel's mistakes, but the people of Judah refused to look at their own sin. In fact, Judah and Jerusalem fell into sin that was worse even than Israel's. The Bible says that Judah became so corrupt, God finally could not endure it any longer. In His eyes, the nation's wound was beyond curing: "There was no remedy" (2 Chronicles 36:16).

Of course, these people lived under the Old Covenant, which required perfect obedience. So when Josiah took the throne, the godly king tried to bring about righteousness in Judah by imposing morality on the people. He did this through governmental decrees and military enforcement. Under Josiah's leadership, a revival took place in Judah. Idols came down, evil was wiped out and the people's conversations focused on the Lord and His work.

Yet this revival was an outward one only. There was not a genuine change in the hearts of the people. It was a shallow revival, full of good works and appearances but not accompanied by true repentance. The people of Judah observed the law and cleaned up their society—but their hearts were not in it. This became evident later, when Josiah died in battle. At that point Judah fell back into gross wickedness. Within a year the people were indulging in idolatry such as the nation had never seen.

Jeremiah was overwhelmed by what he saw taking place among God's people. Adultery and homosexuality had become rampant. The prophet cried, "The land is full of adulterers; for because of swearing the land mourneth; the pleasant places of the wilderness are dried up, and their course is evil, and their force is not right" (Jeremiah 23:10).

Even Judah's priests and prophets had become corrupt. In turn, they corrupted God's house: "For both prophet and priest are profane; yea, in my house have I found their wickedness" (verse 11). These religious leaders should have been warning the people about God's judgment for sin. They should have been faithfully pointing out the difference between the holy and the profane. But, instead, they comforted the people in their sins. Jeremiah listened in disbelief as these false teachers preached peace and prosperity to evildoers, encouraging them in their backsliding: "They say still unto them that despise me, The LORD hath said, Ye shall have peace; and they say unto every one that walketh after the imagination of his own heart, No evil shall come upon you" (verse 17).

Judah's condition became so awful that God compared them to Sodom and Gomorrah, two cities He had wiped off the map:

> Wherefore their way shall be unto them as slippery ways in the darkness: they shall be driven on, and fall therein: for I will bring evil upon them, even the year of their visitation, saith the LORD. And I have seen folly in the prophets of Samaria. . . . I have seen also in the prophets of Jerusalem an horrible thing: they commit adultery, and walk in lies: they strengthen also the hands of evildoers, that none doth return from his wickedness: they are all of them unto me as Sodom, and the inhabitants thereof as Gomorrah.
>
> Jeremiah 23:12–14

Jeremiah could only weep as he saw Judah totally overrun by gross immorality. He cried, "Let mine eyes run down with tears night and day, and let them not cease: for the virgin daughter of my people is broken with a great breach, with a very grievous blow" (Jeremiah 14:17). Finally, the prophet delivered a message of coming judgment: "[God] will now remember their iniquity, and visit their sins" (verse 10).

Same Story, Different Nation

At the time Jeremiah was prophesying judgment, Judah had enjoyed nearly forty years of prosperity. The Lord had honored King Josiah's attempts to bring revival to the land. Yet, even so, a sword of judgment had hung over Judah all that time. You see, God had already determined to send His wrath upon the nation. Why? He could not forgive the bloodshed of innocents committed by the previous generation. Josiah's predecessor, evil King Manasseh, had murdered multitudes of innocents, filling Jerusalem's streets with blood.

Scripture tells us that God will not pardon the shedding of innocent blood in any society:

> Surely at the commandment of the LORD came this [judgment] upon Judah, to remove them out of his sight, for the sins of Manasseh, according to all that he did; and also for the innocent blood that he shed: *for he filled Jerusalem with innocent blood; which the LORD would not pardon.*
>
> 2 Kings 24:3–4, emphasis added

God looked at Manasseh's sin and cried, "I cannot forgive this sin, not ever." Indeed, never in history has God withheld His judgment from a society that has shed great amounts of innocent blood. I believe, for example, that London was destroyed because of its bloodshed in the seventeenth century, and that the Roman Empire fell because of the innocent blood it spilled throughout the centuries.

I also believe that America is next. How can God withhold His wrath from our nation, which has shed the blood of 35 million innocent babies through abortion? Each day in this country, five thousand unborn children are killed. The Lord has raised up prophetic voices in America to cry out warnings of judgment, and many Christians gather in meetings across this country to pray for our nation. But I believe that God's judgment on America has already been determined. Our nation will not be spared.

I believe that, right now, we are enjoying a brief reprieve from God's fiery judgment. It appears our nation is prospering as never before. But I see that the handwriting is on the wall. The Lord is issuing one final mercy call, because He desires to see repentance. He did the same thing with Judah during Josiah's reign. God told that righteous king, "I know you are a praying man and a godly leader. I am going to give your people a brief time of prosperity and peace. So, Josiah, you will not see My judgment fall on Judah during your lifetime. But after you're gone, My judgment will surely come upon this nation, for all its shedding of the blood of innocents."

At that point, Jeremiah received a heavenly revelation of a future Jerusalem. According to the prophet, this new holy city would be ruled by a righteous Branch from the seed of David: "Behold, the days come, saith the LORD, that I will raise unto David a righteous Branch, and a King shall reign and prosper, and shall execute judgment and justice in the earth" (Jeremiah 23:5).

Jeremiah adds that this Branch would save His people, causing them to live in peace: "In his days Judah shall be saved, and Israel shall dwell safely: and this is his name whereby he shall be called, THE LORD OUR RIGHTEOUSNESS" (verse 6).

This is very clearly a prophecy about Jesus Christ, who would secure His people's salvation by His own blood and bring about the heavenly Jerusalem. Indeed, the prophet Zechariah identifies this Branch as Christ—someone who "will remove the iniquity of that land in one day" (Zechariah 3:9). In the midst of a crisis of sin and despair, God gave Jeremiah a fresh revelation of His character—the Lord our righteousness.

Friends, we are living in the very day when "he [Jesus] shall be called, THE LORD OUR RIGHTEOUSNESS" (Jeremiah 23:6). So what does all this mean for us, in practical terms? What is this righteousness He is the Lord of—and how are we to know and understand Jesus in this role?

Grace: From Theory to Reality

You are probably already convinced that every bit of your righteousness comes to you from God, through Jesus' work on the cross. In fact, you may often speak of Christ's righteousness being imputed to you (that is, credited to your account). You may think of your righteousness as being of faith, and not of works or law. You may even forswear trying to work out a righteousness of your own.

Yet as much as we all believe these truths, we often fail to live them out in our daily lives. They have not become a reality to us in the ways that God has intended. Simply put, our lives need to be revolutionized by a revelation of *Jehovah Tsidkenu*. Only as we lay hold of God's concept of righteousness by faith will it become reality.

The apostle Paul confirms this amazing truth. He writes, "Now the righteousness of God without the law is manifested, being witnessed by the law and the prophets; even the righteousness of God which is by faith of Jesus Christ unto all and upon all them that believe" (Romans 3:21–22).

Paul is telling us, in essence, "We are living under a New Testament revelation. It is the revelation of a righteousness that comes from God and not from man. The Lord chose to disclose this revelation to His Old Testament prophets. Every one of them testified of a righteousness to come, which would not be of the law. They said a Messiah was coming to bestow this righteousness on man, rather than man trying to earn it by his own merits. Clearly, the prophets were foreseeing Christ's day."

By its very nature, the Old Covenant points to the revelation of *Jehovah Tsidkenu*, the Lord our righteousness. You see, the law was actually designed to show man the weakness of his flesh. It demanded perfect obedience. Under the law, man had to strive until he came to the point that he died to his flesh. At that point, the work of the law was complete, and the need for *Jehovah Tsidkenu* became clear.

David was one Old Testament witness to *Jehovah Tsidkenu*, the Lord our righteousness. He wrote of the coming Messiah, "In his days shall the righteous flourish; and abundance of peace so long as the moon endureth" (Psalm 72:7).

Coals from the Altar

Isaiah was another witness. He wrote, "Surely, shall one say, in the LORD have I righteousness and strength: even to him shall men come; and all that are incensed against him shall be ashamed. In the LORD shall all the seed of Israel be justified, and shall glory" (Isaiah 45:24–25).

How did Isaiah receive this revelation of *Jehovah Tsidkenu*, the Lord our righteousness? It came to him the hard way—through a deep, trying personal experience.

In the first five chapters of Isaiah, we see the prophet preaching faithfully and walking closely with the Lord. I am convinced that if we had sat under this devoted man's ministry, we would have received the very mind of God. Our souls would have been pierced by sharp arrows of conviction, our lifestyles challenged and changed. By every indication, Isaiah sought God's righteousness with all his heart.

Yet the Lord gave this godly prophet an incredible vision that changed his entire view of righteousness. In this vivid revelation,

Isaiah saw the Lord sitting on His throne, high and holy, lifted up above everything in heaven. The vision was so awesome, so filled with God's holiness and glory, that even the heavenly seraphim surrounding the throne had to cover their eyes and bow in humility. They cried in otherworldly voices, "Holy, holy, holy, is the LORD of hosts" (Isaiah 6:3).

The scene was so heavy with God's holy presence that it drove Isaiah to his knees. He fell face-down, unable to see anything except his own sinfulness. Keep in mind, this was the same man who sought God's righteousness more diligently, and preached His word more faithfully, than perhaps any other person on earth. Yet now this godly prophet found himself crying, "Woe is me! for I am undone" (verse 5). The Hebrew meaning of this phrase is, "I have failed—I perish."

Isaiah then makes an incredible statement. He says, "I am a man of unclean lips" (verse 5). How could this be? Isaiah had been preaching, prophesying—delivering a pure word from heaven with convicting power. Yet now he was so awed by what he witnessed, he called his own words unclean.

Do you get the picture? Isaiah, among the godliest of all the Lord's servants, was stating, "I can't be holy, I can't be righteous. I will never be able to attain that. I have done the best I could—yet, at the end of it all, I have discovered I'm nothing. After all my preaching, all my seeking and searching, I am absolutely undone by the Lord's awesome righteousness. I see clearly now, there is no good thing in me."

Isaiah realized that there was no way he could ever attain true righteousness on his own. Even if he could, it would never stand in the light of God's holiness. So, what could he do? How would he ever be able to enter into God's presence with his head lifted up? It became clear to Isaiah that he would never be accepted in the Lord's eyes unless God Himself took the initiative. The Lord had to come to him in his dead condition and do the work of purging and cleansing him.

Knowing God by Name

God did just that. He directed an angel to take a pair of tongs and remove a live coal from the fiery altar, which represented Christ's sacrifice. The angel then laid the coal on Isaiah's tongue, saying, "Lo, this hath touched thy lips; and thine iniquity is taken away, and thy sin purged" (Isaiah 6:7).

Now Isaiah was acceptable. He was purged and purified, and he could stand before the Lord. He was able to worship along with the seraphim, singing, "Holy, holy, holy is the righteous Lord."

What does this scene mean? God's message to Isaiah, and to every believer today, is crystal clear: We attain true righteousness only by coming to the end of ourselves and by turning to *Jehovah Tsidkenu* to provide it.

Isaiah's justification came by no other means than his words of confession: "Woe is me—I am undone." He speaks for us all when he says, "In my own strength and ability, I am helpless, unable. I can never make myself righteous. Instead, the Lord has purged me by His own blood—He made me righteous by placing that hot coal on my tongue. He did it all for me. I have been purified by His actions, not mine. All I did was tell Him that I am hopeless, lifeless; a dead man without Him."

This is why Isaiah could testify, "Surely, shall one say, in the Lord have I righteousness and strength: even to him shall men come; and all that are incensed against him shall be ashamed. In the LORD shall all the seed of Israel be justified, and shall glory" (Isaiah 45:24–25).

The Clear Call of *Jehovah Tsidkenu*

We have already seen what God revealed to Isaiah about attaining true righteousness. Now, in Jeremiah 23:6, God declared once and for all: "In his days Judah shall be saved, and Israel shall dwell safely: and this is his name whereby he shall be called, THE LORD OUR RIGHTEOUSNESS."

The Lord was saying, "The day is coming when I will send My Righteous One as a Savior to all who accept Him. He is going to secure a people through His own sacrifice. They will know Him as *Jehovah Tsidkenu,* the Lord our righteousness."

The moment God revealed Himself as *Jehovah Tsidkenu,* He declared His utter contempt for every kind of righteousness attempted by flesh. Here in this single verse, proclaimed hundreds of years before the Messiah would appear, God was declaring it a deadly sin for us to try to establish a righteousness of our own. He was saying, in other words, "You must lie down and renounce every effort to be holy through your own strength and abilities. Your Savior alone, the coming Messiah, will be your righteousness."

Even though this is revealed to us in God's Word, we still resist embracing it. We simply do not want to believe there is no good thing in us. We cannot bring ourselves to accept that, in our flesh, we are helpless, undependable and prone to commit the vilest of sins. George Whitefield, the great eighteenth-century preacher, summed up this heart attitude when he wrote, "Self-righteousness is the last idol that is rooted out of the heart."

We may testify, "My righteousness is as filthy rags. I can never earn or merit favor with God," yet we often refuse to submit wholly to the Lord's righteousness. Even when we are convinced that we have surrendered, we tend to backslide into our old striving—into the self-inflicted agony of trying to please God by our own efforts and strength.

The truth is, we can never know true righteousness until we give up hope, once and for all, of ever finding anything good in ourselves that we can bring to the Lord. The righteousness of God is a gift, one that must be credited to us. It comes unearned, undeserved and unmerited. Indeed, the Lord must *initiate* the process by which we receive His righteousness. Then, after giving us a desire to be righteous, He must come to us carrying cleansing fire from His altar, to purge us and make us holy in

His sight. How do we become candidates for this gift of righteousness? It happens only when we admit with true conviction, "Woe is me—I have failed. I am helpless, Lord, finished, undone. Without You, I am a dead man."

What Does God Consider True Righteousness?

In several New Testament passages, Paul gives us some insight into God's definition of righteousness. Each time, Paul speaks of God crediting His own righteousness to Abraham:

- "Abraham believed God, and it was counted unto him for righteousness" (Romans 4:3).
- "Faith was reckoned to Abraham for righteousness" (4:9).
- "Even as Abraham believed God, and it was accounted to him for righteousness" (Galatians 3:6).

Each of these verses refers to one thing that Abraham did to attain true righteousness: He *believed*. Finally, Paul provides the Lord's definition of righteousness:

> [Abraham] staggered not at the promise of God through unbelief; but was strong in faith, giving glory to God; and being fully persuaded that, what he had promised, he was able also to perform. And therefore it was imputed to him for righteousness.
>
> Romans 4:20–22

The Bible could not make this matter any clearer: Righteousness is believing the promises of God, being fully persuaded that He will keep His word. Unrighteousness is unbelief—staggering at His promises, doubting God will do what He promised, and trying to do it ourselves.

Paul explains, "Now to him that worketh is the reward not reckoned of grace, but of debt. But to him that worketh not, but believeth on him that justifieth the ungodly, his faith is counted for righteousness" (Romans 4:4–5). Jesus Himself settles this matter of believing God for our righteousness: "This is the work of God, that ye believe on him whom he hath sent" (John 6:29).

You may object, "But what about the issue of personal obedience? Aren't we supposed to deny ourselves and reject the world? Aren't we commanded to forsake all lusts of the flesh? What about taking up our crosses? Doesn't the Bible say we are to surrender ourselves continually to the Lord, walking in purity and seeking a life that is pleasing to Him?"

In truth, none of these things is possible unless we are fully persuaded that God will keep His covenant promises to us. It all comes down to trusting in His Word. The fact is, our acceptance does not depend on any of these things. We are accepted by God only because we are in Christ. You see, God accepts only one person, Jesus—and, in turn, we are accepted because we believe in His finished work for us on the cross. I repeat Paul's adamant declaration: "Now the righteousness of God without the law is manifested, being witnessed by the law and the prophets; even the righteousness of God which is by faith of Jesus Christ unto all and upon all them that believe" (Romans 3:21–22).

Go ahead—read your Bible through in a year from a sense of duty. Pray for hours each day. Go to church every time the doors are open for services. Wrestle down your besetting sins. Be good, and do good. But I tell you, "Without faith it is impossible to please him" (Hebrews 11:6).

Abraham demonstrated the righteousness that is of faith when he willingly obeyed God's command to sacrifice his own son Isaac. Paul writes of the patriarch, "He believed, even God, who quickeneth the dead, and calleth those things which be not as though they were" (Romans 4:17).

The Lord watched as Abraham raised a knife to slay his son. He heard the cry of faith in Abraham's heart: "Lord, You pledged that this son would be my heir. You said Isaac would be the child of promise who would father entire nations. So, I am fully persuaded that as soon as I slay my boy, You are going to raise him from the dead. I know Your word cannot fail, God. I believe You are able to fulfill everything You have promised to me."

God responded by saying, "That is the righteousness that is of faith, not of works. Abraham is My definition of a righteous man."

David was also a righteous man by God's definition. Paul writes:

> Even as David also describeth the blessedness of the man, unto whom God imputeth righteousness without works, saying, Blessed are they whose iniquities are forgiven, and whose sins are covered. Blessed is the man to whom the Lord will not impute sin.
>
> Romans 4:6–8

David knew that he possessed a blessedness that was not of himself. He realized he was forgiven and accepted before the heavenly Father only because he trusted in God's righteousness.

All He Wants Is Trust

God's only demand of His people has been, "Believe My word. Trust in My promises. Have faith that I will do the impossible for you." We may accept this as a doctrine of our faith and as proper theology. Yet, in practical terms, many of us still believe that God expects more from us than faith. Deep down, we tell ourselves that we do not pray enough, give enough or sacrifice enough. We think God expects us to be more diligent, more disciplined and more faithful. Something inside us keeps insisting, "I can't be righteous before the Lord without more effort, more pain, more struggle." So our flesh jumps in and tries to help God make us righteous. Yet, all along, the only thing God has asked of us is simply to trust Him to do what He has already promised.

Beloved, this is the very kind of unbelief that kept Israel out of the Promised Land. The Israelites' sin was not just idolatry or adultery. It was unbelief—their lack of faith in God to do for them what He had promised.

I often read biographies of Christians whom we consider to be giants of faith. Many of these men and women renounced their worldly possessions, gave away their money to the poor and forsook their careers and friendships. Some chose to live in sparsely furnished homes or single rooms or even small huts. They devoted their time and energy to praying, ministering or helping the poor.

I have always considered such people to be the epitome of righteousness. As I read I would think to myself, *This person was a breed apart from those around him. His walk of faith appears so spiritual, so godly, so devoted. Obviously his is the kind of life that God considers righteous.*

Soon I began to measure my own life against the lives I read about. I became convinced that if only I could live the way these saints did, then my life would be pleasing to the Lord. I just needed to move into a small, simple home, drive an old junker car and get rid of everything except the clothes on my back. If I did these things, then maybe I would grow into a spiritual giant.

It did not take long for me to come to a new line of thinking: *Even if I did these things, I could never measure up to these saints. My life is too full of failures. Those godly people were so meek, so gentle, so dedicated. I am too far below them in this matter of holiness. I will never reach their righteous example. It's just not going to happen for me.*

Over time, I found myself weighed down by a burden of condemnation, and I am convinced that multitudes of other Christians carry around the same heavy weight of guilt. We think that our lives will never measure up to the standard we see in others, but this self-condemnation is the result of judging righteousness by outward appearances. The truth is, some people who led lives of sacrifice remained sinful in God's eyes. Why? They never fully trusted that He would be their righteousness. Instead they relied on their own works and goodness.

God's Word leaves no doubt that the Lord considered His servant David to be a righteous man. Yet if we were to judge David's life by the way we judge our own, we would not think of him as righteous at all. He committed adultery, covered it up, murdered the man whose wife he slept with, then lied about it all (even to a prophet of the Lord). Think about it: Had David been a minister in our day, even the most liberal denomination would not hesitate to defrock him. He brought terrible reproach upon God's name. Today his evil deeds would be splashed all over the front pages and beamed onto TV screens.

But David had a repentant heart and, most of all, he did not trust in his own righteousness but in *Jehovah Tsidkenu,* the Lord, our righteousness. David cried, "Judge me, O Lord my God, according to thy righteousness; and let them not rejoice over me . . . my tongue shall speak of thy righteousness and of thy praise all the day long" (Psalm 35:24, 28).

Falling Helplessly into Righteousness

Perhaps you are like David. You have lost all confidence in your own strength. You are convinced that there is nothing good in you; on the contrary, you see that all you have to present to Him are your struggles and failures. You realize that, unless He accounts to you His righteousness, you are doomed.

So you have turned everything over into the Lord's hands. You are trusting Him, casting all your cares upon Him. You believe in His promises to keep you, protect you and cause you to walk uprightly before Him. You say, "I believe God's Word. He says His name is 'the Lord our righteousness'—and that applies to me. I may not have arrived yet, but I know it is not my job to make that happen—it is the Lord's. I know that, somehow, by His Spirit working in me, He is going to get me there."

God does not want your home, your car, your furniture, your savings or the rest of your possessions. All He wants is your faith—your strong belief in His Word. You may be tempted to look at another person as being more spiritual than you. But that person could actually be struggling hard to keep up an *appearance* of righteousness. As God looks at you, He declares, "There is a righteous man or woman!" Why? Because you have admitted your helplessness and you have trusted in the Lord to give you His righteousness.

Paul tells us that we are counted as righteous in God's eyes for the same reason Abraham was. He writes, "Therefore it was imputed to (Abraham) for righteousness. Now it was not written for his sake alone, that it was imputed to him; but for us also, to whom it shall be imputed, if we believe on him that raised up Jesus our Lord from the dead" (Romans 4:22–24).

You may claim, "I believe this. I have faith in the God who resurrected Jesus." But the question is, Do you trust Him when you are against the wall, or do you dig in to fight it out? Will you decide to believe that the Lord can resurrect your troubled marriage? Do you believe He can bring to life a spiritually dead relative? Do you believe He can deliver you from a harmful habit? Do you believe He can erase your sinful past and restore to you the fullness of life you have lost?

Do you believe that God can take a vessel who is weak, foolish, uneducated—someone despised and looked down upon—and make that person useful in His Kingdom, confounding others who seem wise and mighty? When everything looks hopeless—when you are in an impossible situation with no resources and no hope before you—do you believe God will be your *Jehovah Jireh,* seeing to your need? Do you believe He is committed to keeping His covenant promises to you—and that if even one of His words failed, the heavens would melt and the universe collapse?

Waiting for God . . . Patiently

Scripture shows us why so many Christians give up believing in the Lord's righteousness and go back to trying to establish their own.

Sadly, I am convinced that it is because most people refuse to be patient. They may have plenty of faith, but they do not have the patience required to wait on God to fulfill His promises. Yes, Abraham's faith made him righteous in God's eyes. But Abraham also had to learn patience. Why? He was required to wait a quarter of a century before God fulfilled His word to him.

Of course, Abraham did not possess this patience right away. You remember some of his sinful actions during the long years of dryness before God's promise came. When Abraham agreed with his wife to try and produce their promised son through another woman, that certainly was not an act of faith. Rather, it was a shortcut around faith brought on by fleshly impatience. Eventually God brought Abraham to a place of faith where he inherited the promise, but it happened only after he acquired patience.

Our great need for patience is repeated throughout the book of Hebrews:

- "For when God made promise to Abraham, because he could swear by no greater, he sware by himself . . . *and so, after he had patiently endured, he obtained the promise*" (Hebrews 6:13–15, emphasis added).
- "Be not slothful, but followers of them who through faith and patience inherit the promises" (Hebrews 6:12).
- "For ye have need of patience, that, after ye have done the will of God, ye might receive the promise" (Hebrews 10:36).

Friends, God has given us many wonderful covenant promises—to break every bond of sin, to empower us to defeat all dominion of sin, to give us a new heart, to cleanse and sanctify us and to conform us to the very image of Christ. His Word assures us, "[He] is able to keep you from falling, and to present you faultless before the presence of his glory with exceeding joy" (Jude 24).

God does all of these things for us in His time, according to His divine schedule. He has no deadlines pushing Him, and He ignores all demands for an instant cure-all. True faith demands that we wait patiently on our Lord. Our response to Him should be, "Lord, I believe You are true to Your word. By the power of Your Spirit within me, I am going to wait patiently until You bring these things to pass in my life. My part is to remain in faith, waiting on You."

You may endure awful trials and temptations, and you may hear horrendous lies whispered to you by Satan. At times, you may fail. In fact, you may wonder if you will ever reach the goal. As you are enduring all of these afflictions, simply hold onto faith with patience. Trust that God is at work, keeping His word, being your *Jehovah Tsidkenu*. Even if you do not feel righteous, believe Him and He will look upon you as righteous. He has sworn by oath, "By faith, you will receive the promise."

Your flesh may try to rush in and help. It may urge you to turn back to the Old Covenant system of works to try to establish your own righteousness. You may be afraid that you are too much of a mess and that you have to do something so that God will not be offended. But what you must do is to stand firm, declaring, "Lord, I trust only You. My flesh is pulling at me, but I believe that You will bring me back to faith. You have said that You are able to present me faultless before You, and I believe You. I serve *Jehovah Tsidkenu*—the Lord my righteousness."

seven

Jehovah Shammah

The Lord Is There

The prophet Ezekiel describes a terrifying vision he was given by the Lord. In this supernatural vision, Ezekiel saw God's glory departing from both the Temple and the city of Jerusalem. As the Lord's glory departed, awful judgments began to fall—on the Temple, the city and all of Judah. For many years the prophet had been warning about the coming judgment. Now, as this terrifying vision was unveiled to him, Ezekiel knew without a doubt that he was seeing the prophesied judgments begin to fall.

The vision began with a nearly indescribable chariot. This chariot had "wheels within wheels" and was drawn by legions of cherubim. Evidently the wings of the cherubim provided the physical force that moved the chariot. It was an awesome sight: a supernatural chariot supported by winged creatures from heaven.

As the chariot descended from heaven, Ezekiel saw within it a figure sitting upon a throne. The figure was brilliant in appearance—as bright as a sapphire, the prophet says. We can safely assume this figure was none other than the Lord. The glory that Ezekiel witnessed was the Lord's manifest presence. (The New Testament tells us that Jesus is the brightness and brilliance of the Father's glory. So if we compare Ezekiel's description to other passages in the Old Testament in which the Lord appeared, we can be sure this brilliant figure was Christ.)

Ezekiel saw the cherubim-propelled chariot descend and hover over the Temple. Now the full impact of the chariot's terrible mission began to dawn on Ezekiel: It had come to remove God's *shekinah* glory from the Temple. The Lord was visiting His people in order to withdraw His glory from them.

Ezekiel was alarmed, yet he knew exactly why God was removing His glory. He had seen with his own eyes all the awful things that God's people had done, both in the Temple and throughout the land. In the Temple's outer court, for example, the people had turned away from the holy place. Instead, they faced east to worship the sun. In addition they had allowed all kinds of creeping, crawling creatures into the Temple. Evidently they had been sacrificing snakes, lizards and other reptiles (characteristic of the heathen worship in surrounding countries), and they had neglected to offer the pure sacrifice of lambs. God was saying, "I will no longer tolerate these abominations in My house. I will not allow My glory to coexist with such sin."

Ezekiel watched in horror as the heavenly chariot literally picked up the glory of God, removed it from the holy place and carried it to the Temple door. "Then the glory of the LORD went up from the cherub, and stood over the threshold of the house; and the house was filled with the cloud, and the court was full of the brightness of the LORD's glory" (Ezekiel 10:4). God's glory was on the move. Now it was poised at the door, on the very threshold of leaving the Temple.

Scripture describes one final blast of God's glory—a last shining forth of His presence in the midst of the people: "The sound of the cherubims' wings was heard even to the outer court, as the voice of the Almighty God when he speaketh" (verse 5).

How did God's people react to this awesome display of supernatural power? No one even noticed. The priests and people went about their business, performing all their rituals and activities. How could this be, you ask? These people were obviously incapable of recognizing the departure of God's glory in their midst. They had become so blinded by their selfish, sinful pursuits that they did not realize His presence was about to leave them.

In spite of Ezekiel's warnings over the years, the people of Judah had fallen away from God. The nation was full of idol worship, rebellion and wickedness. The people had given themselves over to all kinds of horrible practices—sensuality, demonic visitations and perverted "worship" with prostitutes. The priests had allowed false prophets to infiltrate the Temple, and these false guides filled the people's minds with empty hopes of peace and prosperity. Ezekiel tried to warn the people about the consequences of their evil practices, but they dismissed him, mocking his words and continuing to indulge themselves.

Judah's blinded condition shows us that it is possible for God's people to lose the Lord's presence and not realize it. They can be deceived by their own sin. This was not the first time such tragic deception had befallen God's people. Scripture says that when God's presence left Samson, he did not realize what had happened: "[Samson] wist not that the LORD was departed from him" (Judges 16:20).

How could this mighty man of God not know that the Lord's Spirit had left him? Like Judah, he was blinded by sin. Samson openly indulged in sensuality, never thinking he would reap any consequences. He had become convinced, "It doesn't matter what kind of lust I indulge in. I can accomplish great exploits for the Lord at any time. I can get back up every time and do the same things for God I've always done."

Are We Blind?

I know of churches that are just like Samson. For years their congregations have indulged in sinfulness, worldliness and apathy. Over those years God has withdrawn His glory from their midst, but the people have no idea that their persistent sin has driven away the Lord's holy presence. Like Samson they remain convinced that "everything in our church is the same as it's always been." So, they attend to business as usual. They engage in dry routines and rituals, going through the motions of their empty religion. But God is no longer with them as He should be, and it does not take long for praying people in this kind of congregation to recognize that something is wrong. Their sensitive hearts tell them something important is missing. Finally, to their horror, the Holy Spirit reveals that He is no longer active in the place. He makes it clear that God has removed His presence from that church because the people have persisted in permissiveness and compromise with sin.

The same holds true of individual believers. Right now multitudes of Christians sit in the laps of their own Delilahs, indulging in blatant disobedience to God's Word. Over time they have become deceived by their sin, just as Samson was. They assume, "I'm still a servant of God. His Spirit is still with me. I can go on as I always have." They do not realize that God's glory has already departed from them. His presence is no longer in their lives, because they have refused to give up their disobedience.

No One Left to Weep

Ezekiel grieved as God finally lifted His glory from Judah's midst.

As God's glory hovered at the Temple door, Ezekiel saw it moving once again. He writes, "Then the glory of the LORD departed from off the threshold of the house, and stood over the cherubim. And the cherubim lifted up their wings, and mounted up from the earth in my sight . . . and the glory of the God of Israel was over them above" (Ezekiel 10:18–19).

The cherubim mounted in an upward surge that seemed to lift God's glory up from the Temple. Next, these angelic beings rose and held the glory above the city, suspended in the sky above the people. This hovering, hesitating image suggests the Lord was reluctant to leave. He seemed to be waiting for a voice to cry as David did: "Don't leave us, Lord! Don't take Your Spirit from our midst. Please return Your holy presence to us."

I imagine Ezekiel screaming in his soul as he beheld this scene. He probably wanted to shout, "Somebody, somewhere—please, get up and cry out to God. Who is willing to stand in the gap? God's glory is on the move, about to be withdrawn from you. You have got to call upon the Lord right now, before it's too late."

But there was no such voice, no outcry, no intercessor. Nobody stepped forward to stand in the gap. So God lifted His glory and removed it from Judah: "The glory of the LORD went up from the midst of the city, and stood upon the mountain which is on the east side of the city" (Ezekiel 11:23). (The mountain Ezekiel describes here was the Mount of Olives.)

How did the people respond once God's glory left them? You might think that the priests would have shut down the Temple and ceased all religious activities. You might think they would have called for a day of mourning and repentance in recognition of what had happened, especially in light of the judgments falling. But the Temple doors did not close—not at all. On the contrary, everything continued just as it always had. Once again the priests and people went about doing all the things they usually did.

Now these sinful people could be much more comfortable about indulging their sin. They had been miserable whenever the Lord's glory was present among them, because it constantly exposed their sin. Now that God's glory was out of the way, conviction was gone. They did not care a bit that the Lord had removed Himself from their midst.

So it is in many churches today. Many dead congregations once enjoyed the Lord's presence in their midst. Their pastors were mighty men of prayer. They stepped into the pulpit each week armed with a pure word from God. But then a compromising pastor came to leadership. Over the years, sin was ignored and standards fell to convenience. Gradually, people closed the doors of their hearts to the Holy Spirit's conviction. Now, all over the world, these congregations are dying. They have turned their eyes away from their sin. They prefer not to allow God's holy conviction to touch them. In all sincerity I believe that this is why old-line denominational churches are closing down at an alarming rate.

A Second Vision

Fourteen years into the Babylonian captivity, Ezekiel received another amazing vision. By this time the spirits of both Israel and Judah were utterly broken. God's people had been in captivity for fourteen years, their pride long since laid in the dust. As they slaved by the rivers of Babylon, they wept as they remembered the glory of Zion. They no longer had anything to sing about. There was nothing in their lives that they wanted to praise God for, so they hung their harps on the willows. They finally faced the fact that God had removed His glory from them years before because they had desecrated His house with idolatry and sin.

The revelation given to Ezekiel at this time was even more amazing than the first. The Holy Spirit took the prophet to a high mountain that overlooked Jerusalem and all of Judah. There God showed Ezekiel another city—one the Lord would build in the future. This city would be glorious beyond all imagination. In fact, its expanse would be so great that it could not be contained within the nation's borders.

God then revealed to Ezekiel yet another incredible vision. This one was a revelation of a great and majestic new Temple. The wondrous structure would be the permanent Temple to which God's glory would return, never to leave again. As the Lord unfolded the revelation of this Temple to Ezekiel, He gave the prophet minute details of its entire construction. He showed him its courts, rooms and chambers, and described the kind of priests who would minister there. What a complex structure the Temple was going to be! It took Ezekiel nine chapters just to outline it.

Because Ezekiel describes the Temple as impossibly huge and majestic, I do not believe God wants us to interpret it as being a literal temple. Rather, it was meant to represent the majestic Kingdom of Christ.

That is not to say that I believe we should try to find symbolism in every detail of this magnificent structure. Even the most astute theologians have gotten lost in a jungle of mystical allusions while trying to interpret the details. That is not what this vision is all about. Ezekiel was not seeing a literal temple. Indeed, there is no evidence anywhere in Ezekiel's writings to suggest this temple was intended to be an actual building.

Nevertheless Christian groups differ on this matter. Some subscribe, for example, to the Orthodox Jewish interpretation that there will be a rebuilt Temple, with animal sacrifices restored to worship practices. They believe that through the Temple's restoration the Jews will turn to the Lord. In my opinion, this belief goes against everything Paul tells us in Galatians. The apostle firmly declares there was only one true Lamb slain from the foundation of the world. That Lamb's sacrifice took place once and for all. In other words, all the animal sacrifices we see in the Old Testament were only types and shadows. They were replaced by the reality of Christ's sacrifice on our behalf. As the author of Hebrews tells us, Jesus' sacrifice is a finished work; therefore, because the blood of bulls and goats cannot forgive sin, such animal sacrifices are now a wasted offering.

Besides, if Ezekiel's vision was a real blueprint, why did the Jews never try to build the structure he described? After all, their captivity ended eventually and they returned to Jerusalem to rebuild the Temple. Yet when this happened, not one detail of Ezekiel's vision was adopted. Why not? It was simply impossible to accomplish, and the people knew it.

If you were to outline the dimensions of the Temple Ezekiel described, including all its environs, it would encompass twice the land mass of Judah. This in itself made such a structure impossible to build. In addition, how could any human being devise the kind of river Ezekiel described—one that originated in the Temple and increased in volume as it ran outward for miles? Ezekiel said this river began at a person's ankles, then rose to the knees and finally became deep enough to swim in. What human could construct such a flowing body of water out of the midst of a building?

It is obvious to me that Ezekiel was seeing the heavenly Jerusalem. He was describing a holy city coming down out of heaven, which the New Testament calls the Church of Jesus Christ. Ezekiel was being given a vision of the New Jerusalem—the mother of all believers, to whom the glory of God would return and never depart. This remarkable vision of Christ's Church is strikingly similar to a city described in Psalm 46:4–5: "There is a river, the streams whereof shall make glad the city of God, the holy place of the tabernacles of the most High. God is in the midst of her; she shall not be moved: God shall help her, and that right early."

The Jews may once again rebuild the Temple in Jerusalem, but God's glory will not be in it unless Christ is there. I have no doubt that Ezekiel was seeing the worldwide, spiritual city that is to be our Lord's habitation forever. This is the true Temple—the Body consisting of every born-again believer, a tabernacle that could not possibly be made with human hands.

Paul echoes this in his letters to the Corinthians. He says God's Temple is embodied in our physical beings: "Know ye not that ye are the temple of God, and that the Spirit of God dwelleth in you?" (1 Corinthians 3:16). "Ye are the temple of the living God; as God hath said, I will dwell in them, and walk in them; and I will be their God, and they shall be my people" (2 Corinthians 6:16).

A Hope and a Warning

What can we learn from Ezekiel's vision? I believe the Lord wants us to understand two things.

1. A Revelation

The prophet envisioned the glory of God returning and a revelation of *Jehovah Shammah* coming forth.

Ezekiel writes, "Then brought he me the way of the north gate before the house: and I looked, and, behold, the glory of the LORD filled the house of the LORD: and I fell upon my face" (Ezekiel 44:4). This amazing new Temple was a gigantic structure, filled from one end to the other with the Lord's brilliant glory. When Ezekiel laid eyes on it, he fell on his face.

I would not even begin to try to put symbolic terms to all the things Ezekiel describes in this vision. But I believe the various rooms and chambers that make up this glorious Temple could represent the various peoples of the world. I think Ezekiel was seeing all the races becoming one under the roof of God's house. He writes, "The name of the city from that day shall be, The LORD is there" (Ezekiel 48:35).

The literal Hebrew words for this last phrase are *Jehovah Shammah*. Ezekiel was saying, in other words, "These people will be known by God's presence in them and upon them. It will be said of this Temple, 'God is there. The presence of the Lord is with them.'"

2. A Guardianship

The Lord told Ezekiel to guard the gates to this new house, in which the glory of God would now abide. It is as if God was saying: "I will not put up with the abominations I endured in the old Temple. You have to warn the people about this."

We have already read of all the awful things the people brought into the Temple during the old order. God said the priests during that time "ministered unto them before their idols, and caused the house of Israel to fall into iniquity" (Ezekiel 44:12). In turn, the fleshly worshipers clamored for leaders who would encourage their idolatry, confirming them in their sins. The result was that both ministers and lay people polluted God's house with corrupt worship.

Now the Lord was putting a stop to all of that. He told Ezekiel, "Thus saith the Lord GOD; No stranger, uncircumcised in heart, nor uncircumcised in flesh, shall enter into my sanctuary" (verse 9). God was instructing the prophet, "Ezekiel, I have set guards over these Temple gates. No corrupt leader or ungodly person will enter. No one who has an uncircumcised heart can be permitted into My holy place. I am going to have a holy Body inhabiting My last-days' Church. I will not allow any polluters to corrupt this house. No one with an unclean heart can stand and minister before Me."

Is This Your Church?

What does this mean for us in these last days? It means Satan will not be allowed to invade the holy Temple where God's glory dwells. The Lord has proclaimed that His pastors and believers will be full of His glory. He will not allow any ungodly, unclean person to minister in this new Temple. He told Ezekiel, "They shall not come near unto me, to do the office of a priest unto me, nor to come near to any of my holy things, in the most holy place" (Ezekiel 44:13).

You may wonder, "But there are all kinds of corruption and pollution in churches today. Backslidden ministers continue to condone the sins in their flock. Some denominations are ordaining homosexual pastors. Church leaders are excusing adultery, mocking the reality of heaven and hell and denying the Scriptures to be the inerrant Word of God. How could anyone believe that the Church has not been corrupted?"

You are right to recognize these awful things going on in the Church. Such ministers and leaders are wolves in sheep's clothing. They are seducers, flatterers, compromised shepherds who refuse to show the people their sins. Because they do not believe in the authority of God's Word, they receive no fresh word from Him. When they stand in the pulpit to preach, they simply repeat other men's sermons. These godless men of the cloth minister not to God, but to the idolatry and wickedness of the people—and they are causing their flocks to fall even deeper into iniquity.

I tell you, these shepherds will never minister in the holy Temple Ezekiel saw coming. God has already declared that the days of mixture are no more. All the foolishness and abominations we see going on, therefore, are not a part of God's true house. These awful things are part of the old, dead order, and God has forsaken that order. He has already declared that it has no place in His holy sanctuary, where *Jehovah Shammah* abides.

No doubt you have heard this cry among concerned believers: "The church has totally lost its influence in society! It has lost all of its political clout, and it is completely irrelevant in the eyes of young people. The perception we get through the media and from our nation's leaders is that our churches are merely incidental to people's lives."

If you think the carnal church has lost its power and authority on earth, you can be sure it has even less influence in heaven. The backslidden church in America today certainly has no power with God. I believe that over the years it has become a stench in His nostrils. The Lord has washed His hands of it all, refusing to have anything to do with a self-satisfied, lukewarm church. One day soon, He is going to spew the backslidden churches out of His mouth.

There is only one Church our Lord recognizes. His true Temple—His holy sanctuary, where His glory abides—consists of a righteous ministry and a faithful, God-hungry people. This is not the visible, structured church system. Rather, this Church is made up of a body here, a body there—in Africa, India, China, the United States and other nations. In these holy houses, the uncircumcised in heart are not allowed to minister, and they never will be. Instead, God has a people who are righteous before Him and who will remain so until Jesus comes.

What is the name of this Church? It is known as "The Lord is there"—the Church of *Jehovah Shammah.*

A New Order of Priests

Ezekiel tells us that the ministers in the glorious new Temple will consist of an entirely new order. He describes this new priesthood by first telling us what the old order was like. God says through the prophet:

> The Levites that are gone away far from me, when Israel went astray, which went astray away from me after their idols; they shall even bear their iniquity. Yet they shall be ministers in my [old] sanctuary, having charge at the gates of the house, and ministering to the house: they shall slay the burnt offering and the sacrifice for the people, and they shall stand before them to minister unto them. Because they ministered unto them before their idols, and caused the house of Israel to fall into iniquity;

therefore have I lifted up mine hand against them, saith the LORD God, and they shall bear their iniquity. And they shall not come near unto me, to do the office of a priest unto me, nor to come near to any of my holy things, in the most holy place: but they shall bear their shame, and their abominations which they have committed.

Ezekiel 44:10–13

In this passage the Lord outlines all the abominations of the old order. They may continue with their rituals and programs, but God swears that they will not be ministering to Him, nor will they "come near Him." Then He begins to describe the new Temple priesthood who will lead and serve His people:

But the priests the Levites, the sons of Zadok, that kept the charge of my sanctuary when the children of Israel went astray from me, they shall come near to me to minister unto me, and they shall stand before me to offer unto me the fat and the blood, saith the LORD God: they shall enter into my sanctuary, and they shall come near to my table, to minister unto me, and they shall keep my charge.

Ezekiel 44:15–16

The Hebrew name *Zadok* means "right" or "righteous." Ezekiel is referring here to a man named Zadok who served as priest during King David's reign. This righteous man never wavered in his faithfulness to David or to the Lord. He stood by the king and by God's Word through thick and thin. It did not matter whether David was reigning powerfully from Israel's throne or fleeing the holy city to escape an uprising led by his rebellious son Absalom. Zadok always remained loyal to David because he knew the king was the Lord's anointed.

You see, not every priest had this attitude. Abiathar was also a priest under David's reign. When Absalom overthrew his father and pronounced himself king, Abiathar forsook David and joined the rebellion. The ordeal revealed Abiathar's faithless heart. Later, when David's son Solomon ascended the throne, he banished Abiathar to the wilderness. He told the priest, "You have been faithless in your role as a priest unto the Lord. You no longer have any part in the Temple ministry."

Because Zadok remained faithful through everything, he came to represent a ministry distinguished by its faithfulness to the Lord. Indeed, Zadok was a prime example of a true minister of God—separated from this world, shut in with the Lord, consistently hearing from heaven. Such a minister recognizes his main work as prayer: seeking God daily, communing constantly with the Holy Spirit and ministering to Jesus. Moreover, this kind of minister cannot be bought at any price. While other ministers chase after every religious fad, this shepherd remains faithful to the Lord and to his priestly service in the Temple.

Such is the Zadok priesthood, and the Lord has many Zadokites in His Temple service today. You will not find these shepherds preaching out of selfish motivation. Zadokites would not dare to preach a lifeless sermonette or some message that has not come from God's heart. Instead, these ministers come to the pulpit straight from their secret closets of prayer. They are faithful to stand before the Lord before they ever stand before the congregation. They spend precious hours in the Lord's presence until they are saturated with a message that has been burned into their souls. When they emerge from God's presence, they are able to speak straight to the people's hearts, and their messages get down to where people live because they have come directly from God's throne.

The Lord says of the Zadok priesthood, "These ministers will enter My sanctuary and stand before Me. They shall come near to My table and minister to Me. They shall keep My charge. I will be faithful to lead and direct them, and I will give them My word for My people."

The Zadok Calling Is for Every Believer

In the new, last-days' sanctuary, members of the Zadok priest-hood know that their central work is to minister to the Lord. This ministry includes every lover of Jesus who desires to walk in righteousness. Indeed, we see the "priesthood of believers" echoed throughout the books of the New Testament. The apostle John tells us: "[He] hath made us kings and priests unto God and his Father. . . . And hast made us unto our God kings and priests" (Revelation 1:6; 5:10).

Likewise, the apostle Peter writes: "Ye also, as lively stones, are . . . an holy priesthood, to offer up spiritual sacrifices, accept-able to God by Jesus Christ. . . . But ye are a chosen generation, a royal priesthood, an holy nation, a peculiar people; that ye should shew forth the praises of him who hath called you out of darkness into his marvellous light" (1 Peter 2:5, 9).

You may not have ministerial credentials from any church body. You may never have been to seminary. You may never have preached a sermon. But you are just as called and ordained to serve in the Zadok priesthood as the most well-known preacher or evangelist. Both Testaments make it abundantly clear: Each of us is to hold the office of priest and to perform a priest's duties.

How do you do this? You do it by ministering primarily unto the Lord. You offer up sacrifices to Him—sacrifices of praise, of service, of turning over to Him all your heart, soul, mind and strength. He has called you to be part of His royal priesthood; therefore, you are to minister to others only after you have ministered to Him.

This means you are not to show up at God's house each week empty and dry, hoping some message from the preacher will fire you up. No, you are to come prepared to minister to the Lord with a heart of praise. To do that, you need to be shut up with Him often—in your home, on your job, everywhere. You have been set apart as His minister—a faithful Zadok priest who calls on His name regularly, trusting fully in His righteousness and not your own.

Unless you are a priest in this Zadok ministry—unless you stand before God's table daily, ministering to Him—you cannot be a member of the Church of *Jehovah Shammah*. You may spend all your time supporting church activities and meeting others' needs. But unless you are a Zadok priest in every aspect of your life, all those other activities amount to nothing.

To be a member of God's true Church, you must be known by the name of *Jehovah Shammah*. Others must be able to say of you, "It is clear to me that the Lord is with this person. Every time I see him, I sense the presence of Jesus. His life truly reflects the glory of God."

This cannot be said of many Christians today. If we are honest we have to admit that we do not sense the Lord's sweet presence in each other very often. Why? The majority of Christians spend their time involved in good religious activities—prayer groups, Bible studies, outreach ministries—and that is all very commendable. But many of these same Christians spend little—if any—time ministering to the Lord in the secret closet of prayer.

The Lord's presence simply cannot be faked. This is true whether it applies to an individual's life or to a church body. When I speak of God's presence I am not talking about some kind of spiritual aura that mystically surrounds a person or that "comes down" in a church service. I am talking about the result of a simple but powerful walk of faith. Whether that is manifested in a Christian's life or in an entire congregation, it causes people to take note. They tell themselves, *This person has been with Jesus* or *This congregation truly believes what it preaches.*

Here is my point: It takes much more than a righteous Zadok pastor to produce a *Jehovah Shammah* church. It takes a righteous people who spend time with God. If a stranger comes out of a church service and says, "I felt the presence of Jesus there," you can be sure it was not just because of the preaching or worship.

It was because a righteous Zadok congregation had entered God's house, and the Lord's glory was abiding in their midst.

I have many minister friends who are godly, righteous Zadokite ministers. These individuals are faithful to preach the pure word of God. But not all of their congregations are of this royal priesthood. In such churches, the pastor's sermons are ignored. The minister can see the apathy in his people; few in his church are growing in Christ. No one outside the church is getting saved. It cannot be said of that church body, *Jehovah Shammah*—the Lord is there.

These pastor friends weep many righteous tears over the apathy of their congregations. There can be no life in those houses, however, without holy Zadok congregations who minister regularly to the Lord in their own lives.

Every true shepherd of the Lord wants people to walk out of his church saying, "Surely the Lord is in this place." Yet this ought to be the burden not just of the pastor, but of every Zadok priest in the house. It can happen only if there is a body of Zadokites in the pews, people who come to God's house after they have been with Jesus at home. No church can be more alive than the people who attend it. Dead believers make for dead churches.

A Special Fruit of the Lord's Presence

Ezekiel says that when God's glory is present, His people will be taught to discern between what is holy and what is unholy. As the Lord revealed His vision of the new Temple, He told Ezekiel: "They shall teach my people the difference between the holy and profane, and cause them to discern between the unclean and the clean" (Ezekiel 44:23). Whenever a body of godly servants seek to minister to the Lord, God gives them eyes to see what is of the Spirit and what is of the flesh. They recognize the difference between the holy and the profane.

So what does the name *Jehovah Shammah* mean to us today? It means that others should be able to say of us, "I see Christ in that person." We can no longer try to fake God's presence in our lives. Others will simply know if He is present when they encounter us. They may not know exactly what they are sensing—but their hearts will tell them, "That person is filled with Jesus."

eight

Jehovah Rohi

The Lord My Shepherd

We are all familiar with the Twenty-third Psalm. Its comforting message is well known even among non-believers. This renowned poem was written by King David, and its most famous passage is contained in the opening verse: "The LORD is my shepherd; I shall not want."

The Hebrew word David uses for *want* in this verse indicates "lack." David is saying, in other words, "I shall not lack anything." When we combine this meaning with the first part of the verse, we find that David is saying, "The Lord leads, guides and nourishes me. Because of that, I have no lack."

In this brief verse David gives us yet another reflection of the Lord's character and nature. The literal Hebrew translation of the first part of this verse is *Jehovah Rohi*. It means "the Lord my shepherd."

David continues to develop this idea of the Lord as a shepherd throughout the rest of the psalm. In the next verse he writes, "He maketh me to lie down in green pastures: he leadeth me beside the still waters" (Psalm 23:2).

What an idyllic picture! As we read this verse we often envision a flock of fleecy, white sheep dotting a tranquil green landscape. These well-fed creatures graze on the plentiful grass surrounding them in a vast pasture. Or they lie about on a lush green carpet of grass, napping peacefully. Overhead, the sun is shining brightly. On the nearby hillside, a grove of tall, leafy trees sways gently in the breeze, and down below a beautiful woods is reflected in a pool of cool, clear water.

The whole scene seems so pleasant, peaceful and carefree. Not a creature in sight has a care in the world. Why? Because sitting on the plush grass of the gently sloping hillside, overseeing all that goes on below, is a shepherd. This shepherd is a picture of calm. He gazes out at his flock occasionally to make sure all is well. The shepherd does not hear a single cry or sigh from the peaceful fold in his care. Instead he sees below him a contented flock of rested, satisfied sheep, creatures who fully enjoy their peaceful surroundings.

But something is wrong with this picture—namely that life is nothing like this image of idyllic existence! It is my sincere belief that this tranquil picture is not the image David intended to put forth in Psalm 23.

Consider how even the saintliest group of God's people is a motley bunch. With that in mind, I want to paint for you another picture of the sheepfold David describes here. Yes, sheep are lying about in green grass beside still waters. But according to Isaiah, this flock includes lambs that are frail, weak and unsteady. Some are barely able to walk. Others are in deep pain. A few are pregnant. Still others have to nurse their restless young.

Isaiah writes, "He shall feed his flock like a shepherd: he shall gather the lambs with his arm, and carry them in his bosom, and shall gently lead those that are with young" (Isaiah 40:11). Isaiah is speaking here, of course, of Christ, our *Jehovah Rohi*. Our Lord Jesus is our shepherd. He came to tend not just healthy, strong sheep but also those who are sick, broken, diseased and weak.

God condemned Israel's ministers because they did not fulfill this role for the sheep under their care. It was so important in the Lord's eyes that He voiced His displeasure through every major prophet:

> The diseased have ye not strengthened, neither have ye healed that which was sick, neither have ye bound up that which was broken, neither have ye brought again that which was driven away, neither have ye sought that which was lost.
>
> Ezekiel 34:4

> My sheep wandered through all the mountains, and upon every high hill: yea, my flock was scattered upon all the face of the earth, and none did search or seek after them.
>
> Ezekiel 34:6

> My people hath been lost sheep . . . they have forgotten their resting place.
>
> Jeremiah 50:6

> All we like sheep have gone astray.
>
> Isaiah 53:6

Note the last verse. Whom is Isaiah talking about here, when he says we all have gone astray? He is talking about you, about me—about every person who belongs in the Lord's sheepfold. Do not think the prophet was exaggerating for effect. Mark it down: Every sheep in the shepherd's fold has gone astray. Yet each of us is still in the fold because our gracious, merciful and loving Shepherd has come after us and found us.

Just look around you for a moment, at all the sheep you know in the Church of Jesus Christ. Examine yourself, your believing friends, your pastor, the people in your congregation. What kind of flock are you? Are you all lying down in green pastures, drinking pure cool water? Are you all perfectly contented, healthy, happy, peaceful?

No way! You have in your midst baby believers who keep stumbling and falling. At times you wonder if they are ever going to be strong enough to walk straight. Others are forced to carry their young. Their offspring are not yet born again and walking on their own. Often these sincere believers are reduced to tears because of their young ones' straying.

Others among us are sick and diseased. They have drunk polluted water from the well of some false teacher. Still others are hobbling around, wounded by life's hardships. Some have a crippled, bleeding leg that their shepherd had to pull out of a lion's mouth. Others were crippled by evil habits and lusts. Still others among us are naked—shorn or fleeced by false shepherds who took them for everything they had.

All of these sick, broken sheep have been brought back to the fold by the Shepherd Himself. Some were so maimed, disabled, hurt and disoriented that Jesus had to put them on His shoulders and carry them all the way back to the flock.

That is the role of our great Shepherd. Several passages of Scripture describe this wonderful trait of our Lord even more clearly:

For thus saith the Lord God; Behold, I, even I, will both search my sheep, and seek them out.

Ezekiel 34:11

The sheep Ezekiel describes here have obviously wandered away, yet the Lord still calls them His sheep. He willingly goes to rescue them.

> As a shepherd seeketh out his flock in the day that he is among his sheep that are scattered; so will I seek out my sheep, and will deliver them out of all places where they have been scattered in the cloudy and dark day.
>
> Ezekiel 34:12

These are sheep who have been through deep, dark passages—the experience of every devoted follower of Jesus. We all have faced dark times in our walks with the Lord.

> I will feed them in a good pasture, and upon the high mountains of Israel shall their fold be: there shall they lie in a good fold, and in a fat pasture shall they feed upon the mountains of Israel. I will feed my flock, and I will cause them to lie down, saith the Lord GOD.
>
> Ezekiel 34:14–15

Here we see an image repeated from Psalm 23. Once again, the Lord tells us that He causes His sheep to lie down.

> I will seek that which was lost, and bring again that which was driven away, and will bind up that which was broken, and will strengthen that which was sick. . . . Therefore will I save my flock, and they shall no more be a prey; and I will judge between cattle and cattle. And I will set up one shepherd over them, and he shall feed them, even my servant David; he shall feed them, and he shall be their shepherd.
>
> Ezekiel 34:16, 22–23

Once again, God speaks clearly about setting up one true Shepherd to watch over His people. He is referring, of course, to Christ. Jesus is the Good Shepherd who promises to feed His flock.

The Hebrew phrase for *maketh* in Psalm 23:1 means, literally, to "induce" or "compel." In other words, the Shepherd compels His sheep—that is, He makes them—to lie down. The literal meaning of this verse is, "He interrupts me to make me lie down."

Many in the flock of Christ today are ready to lie down. These sheep are sick, diseased, weary, fainting—and they know it. They are mud-stained, wounded, bleeding and hurting. They are in such bad shape that the Shepherd Himself has to recover them. After He carries them back He instructs them to lie down, and they comply happily.

Do you get the picture? When David writes, "He restoreth my soul" (Psalm 23:3), he is speaking of healing and restoration. He is describing a flock of bruised and battered sheep lying in a green valley. Whenever we are sick and hurting, bruised and wounded, our Shepherd Jesus carries us to a place where we can be healed. There, in the valley of His love, He operates on us. He binds up the wounded, strengthens the weak, brings health to the sick and renews the frail.

Sometimes, however, it is not easy for our Shepherd to make us "lie down." Often our flesh resists. We do not want to submit wholly to the Lord and be utterly dependent on His mercy and love. Instead we tell ourselves that we have to tough it out, to sweat out our own failings and weaknesses. Rather than turning to Him by faith and resting in His power and grace, we limp off to some secluded place to lick our wounds and try to recover on our own.

As we lie there in our own dark covering, we try to figure everything out. We wonder how we ever could have gotten so muddy and become so wounded. We ask ourselves how we ever got to this place to begin with. We question, "Where did that temptation come from? How was the enemy able to bruise me so badly? What got me into this awful mess? I've got to do something to pull myself out."

Every one of us has had these kinds of thoughts. But the truth is that we will never figure it out. This is exactly what David wants to address in Psalm 23. He is describing a Shepherd who comes after us, dwells in our midst and causes us to lie down while we depend on Him for healing and cleansing.

Jehovah Rohi is not some doting, passive shepherd. He is not a hireling—someone who just provides food and guidance. He does not merely point us toward the grassy pasture and pools of water and say, "There's what you need. Go and get it." Nor does He turn a blind eye to our needs. He does not walk the other way when He hears our cries for help and sees us in trouble. No, He knows every pain we endure, every tear we shed and every hurt we feel. He knows when we are too weary to go another step. He knows just how much we can take. Most of all, He knows how to rescue us and bring us to a place of healing.

Our Shepherd will not allow us to steal away to some secret place where we try to nurse our own wounds. He knows we will bleed to death that way. He comes to take us back, clutching us to His bosom, carrying us through every dark place, leading us back to the green valley where His fold lies. Once there, He tells us, "Lay aside all your fleshly dreams and schemes. Just lie down in My grace now. Do it in faith. This is a time for you to be restored."

Fleecy and Trouble-Free?

I would not know what to do if I were part of a flock where the sheep smiled all day long, showing off pearly white teeth. I do not know if I could handle going to a church where nobody ever cried or experienced pain. I would go crazy if I lived among people who were never sick, never in need, never tempted, never depressed, never downcast or discouraged. If I were mixed in with that kind of flock, I would be a complete misfit, a black sheep. I would be miserable because my life is not like that at all.

I get downcast at times. I go through periods of discouragement. I have experienced times of great confusion. Do not misunderstand: I do have God's peace, but I do not carry a toothpaste grin everywhere I go. Why? Because I have been through the mill, and the trials of life do not exactly make me gleeful.

I have preached thousands of sermons in my lifetime. I have written many books. I have worn out several Bibles in my studies. But I have also shed a river of tears. I have been up on the mountaintops and down in the valleys. I have been through times of testing, trial and sorrow, and on many occasions God has had to come after me. He has had to pick me up, bind up my wounds and give me a bath.

David asked, "Thou art the God of my strength: why dost thou cast me off? Why go I mourning because of the oppression of the enemy?" (Psalm 43:2). This man could not help wondering why he faced such trouble from his enemies. Yet David identifies what his trouble was: "This is an oppression of the enemy."

I know exactly what David was talking about. Every time I set out to do something I believe will have an impact for eternity on people's lives, I can predict what is going to happen. The devil is going to come in like a flood and seek to overwhelm me. Every time I plan to write a book, for instance, I have to prepare myself for the enemy's attacks.

Then, at other times, I experience great physical and mental oppression for no apparent reason. I believe this is just what David was going through when he wrote this verse. He had been assailed by something unexplainable, some oppression of soul that had no clear origin. He had no idea why it was happening. That is why he asked God why he felt so cast off. Something inexplicable had overcome him, and he had no idea what to do about it.

Perhaps you have been through this. You woke up one day with a cloud of depression hovering over you. You had no idea where it came from or why it fell upon you. You thought, *I've never felt this down or condemned in my life. Why is this happening to me now? What's going on?* You examined your heart endlessly but you could not get to the bottom of what you were going through or why.

I believe every true follower of Jesus faces this ordeal. We know David was a true man of God, yet he was unable to explain the sudden despair that flooded his soul. Moreover, it came upon him at a time when his soul was hungering deeply for the Lord. David was well acquainted with oppression. At various times he had been physically wounded, diseased in body, broken in spirit, cast off of Israel's throne, driven out of Jerusalem, scattered to the hills and lost. He also was corrupted by grievous sins and powerful, overwhelming lusts. At times David was forced to wander across the land, fleeing across valleys, hiking up hillsides and hiding in caves.

But David had a caring, loving Shepherd. Each time David was battered and wounded, *Jehovah Rohi* went after him, picked him up and carried him to a quiet place of rest. Then the Lord made David lie down so his soul could be restored.

God had to keep doing this with David throughout his lifetime. You see, David *was* one of those sheep he describes as lying in green pastures beside still waters. That is right: The sheepfold mentioned in Psalm 23 was David's own flock, and this was no one-time scene for the king of Israel. It happened over and over.

God's sheep are no different today. Time after time our Shepherd comes after us, fetches us and takes us to a place of rest. He continually makes us lie down for a time of healing and restoration. Yet, somehow, we so easily move away from the Lord's rest. We do not always hold to the truths we learn about His grace and peace, and soon we find ourselves wandering and straying all over again.

We fail to realize that the Lord's rest is like the food with which we nourish our bodies daily: We cannot retain its value unless we keep coming back to the table. We have to accept that being shepherded by God is a process that He must take us through many times during the course of our Christian walk.

The Lord says in Exodus 29:45, "I will dwell among the children of Israel, and will be their God." The Hebrew word for *dwell* is *shekinah,* meaning "to abide" or "to settle down beside." This word signifies more than a passing presence. It implies a permanent one—a presence that never leaves. In short, the *shekinah* glory of God is not a fleeting imprint that disappears from our hearts like invisible ink. It is something God imprints permanently on our souls. It is His very near and eternal presence.

The picture here is glorious: Our Shepherd offers to come to us in the midst of our pain and depressed condition, and to sit by our side. He promises to bind up our wounds and strengthen the parts of us that have become sick and diseased. That is the *shekinah* glory of God! The abiding, everlasting presence of the Lord. In fact, we often experience it the strongest when we are in the midst of trouble. Our great Shepherd tells us, "I want to restore you, and I am going to do it by being present with you, even in the valley and shadow of death. My presence will be with you through everything the devil throws at you. Even if you try to run from Me, I am going to chase after you. And when I catch you, I am going to take you in My arms and carry you back to My rest. Then I will bind up your wounds and heal all your sicknesses."

Jehovah Rohi Knows His Sheep

Scripture tells us more about our one true Shepherd:

- Jesus states, "I am the good shepherd, and know my sheep, and am known of mine" (John 10:14).

- Paul writes, "The Lord knoweth them that are his" (2 Timothy 2:19).
- Christ declares, "My sheep hear my voice, and I know them, and they follow me: and I give unto them eternal life; and they shall never perish, neither shall any man pluck them out of my hand" (John 10:27–28).

Simply put, our great Shepherd knows who His sheep are. David was familiar with this aspect of the Lord's character because he had experienced it personally. Throughout the Psalms, we read:

- "He knoweth our frame" (Psalm 103:14).
- "He knoweth the secrets of the heart" (Psalm 44:21).
- "The LORD knoweth the thoughts of man" (Psalm 94:11).

David was saying, "The Lord knows what I'm really like, deep down." David realized that God knew how his heart often strayed from the Shepherd's divine love and rest, and yet God still loved him.

By his own admission David was a man whose iniquities piled up so high that they went over his head. As he shouldered the long list of his trespasses, David said it became a burden too heavy for him to carry (see Psalm 38:4). He stated, "There is no soundness [rest] in my flesh because of thine anger; neither is there any rest in my bones because of my sin" (Psalm 38:3).

Do these sound like the words of a healthy, fleecy-white, strong and obedient sheep? Hardly. David writes:

My wounds stink and are corrupt because of my foolishness. I am troubled; I am bowed down greatly; I go mourning all the day long. For my loins are filled with a loathsome disease: and there is no soundness in my flesh. I am feeble and sore broken:

I have roared by reason of the disquietness of my heart. LORD, all my desire is before thee; and my groaning is not hid from thee. My heart panteth, my strength faileth me: as for the light of mine eyes, it also is gone from me.

Psalm 38:5–10

This was obviously the cry of a troubled man. As David acknowledged, "My sins are not hid from thee" (Psalm 69:5). But God's knowledge was not limited to David's evil thoughts, foolishness and evil tendencies. The Lord also knew that His servant had a tender, contrite heart. We see evidence of this in David's refusal to hide or excuse his sins. God knew that David would always declare his iniquity and be sorry for his sin (see Psalm 38:18).

Like David, I have learned this glorious aspect of the Lord's character through experience. I have realized that God knows all of my frailties, weaknesses, jealousies, doubts and failings. I have also learned that He sees my heart and He knows that, like David, I will not hide my sins from Him. Instead, I will confess them openly to my Shepherd. How have I come to do this? I have learned that, in spite of all my iniquities and failures, my Lord loves me.

The Valley of the Shadow of Death

If you have not experienced the dark, perplexing times David faced, I question whether or not you are leading a very spiritual life. Have you never been to the same dry place where David found himself? Have you never thought that the reason everything was going wrong in your life was because God was mad at you? Have you never feared you had lost His favor by grieving Him? If not, you must be living in some kind of spiritual la-la land! I know exactly what David was going through. At times during my decades of walking with the Lord I have thought my faith was unshakable. I have been convinced I would always trust the Lord, no matter what. But then I would be hit with a time of deep testing, and soon the old doubts would begin to creep up on me.

Even Jesus experienced this dark night of the soul. For a brief moment at Gethsemane, and later on the cross, an awful thought crossed His mind: "Why, Father? What have I done? Why do I feel You have turned Your face from Me? How long will You hide?"

At times our ministry has faced financial crunches and, like David, I took counsel with my own heart. I panicked, suddenly scheming up plans to deliver our ministry from its circumstances. I started the days by planning cutbacks here, cutbacks there. Then I stayed up nights brainstorming ideas to raise funds. I complained to everyone around me. I accused the Lord of letting me down. I almost gave up.

But then an avalanche of mail would pour in. Maybe it had been backed up at the post office for a few days. Or maybe it had just been mailed in, even as I paced through the night, worrying and scheming. Each time this happened I was painfully humbled, crying, "Lord, forgive me. What a dunce I am! Why didn't I trust You? Why did I ever doubt Your faithfulness?"

In Psalm 119, after writing 175 "spiritually correct" verses extolling God's Word and faithfulness, David makes a surprising admission.

After exalting God's Word at length, David concludes Psalm 119 with this verse: "I have gone astray like a lost sheep; seek thy servant" (verse 176).

David is saying, in essence, "Please, Lord, seek me out, the way a shepherd searches for a lost sheep. In spite of all my biblical knowledge, preaching and long history with You, somehow I have strayed from Your love. I have lost the rest I once had in You. All my plans have failed, and now I realize that I am totally helpless. Come to me, Father. Seek me out in this awful, dark place. I cannot find You on my own. You must find me. I still believe Your word is true."

David knew he had strayed from God's rest. He knew the Lord's love should have been imprinted on his heart during his previous crises. But now, once again, he had forgotten about God's love for him. So he cried out to the Lord, begging Him to seek out His lost servant.

The Shepherd came after David once again and, as David heard his name called, he was comforted. He realized, "My Shepherd knows me by name." David found himself being led down the hill into the green valley. When he reached the green pasture below, *Jehovah Rohi* said to him, "Lie down now. Go to sleep and rest your weary soul. Don't worry—I'll be at work, taking care of everything."

Now David testified once more:

I have trusted in thy mercy; my heart shall rejoice in thy salvation. I will sing unto the LORD, because he hath dealt bountifully with me.

Psalm 13:5–6

I cried unto the LORD with my voice, and he heard me out of his holy hill. Selah. I laid me down and slept; I awaked; for the LORD sustained me. I will not be afraid of ten thousands of people, that have set themselves against me round about.

Psalm 3:4–6

It is important to note here that David's circumstances had not changed. In fact, Scripture says the enemies who troubled David had only increased (see Psalm 3:1). But David had been restored to God's love. Now he could say, "Salvation [deliverance] belongeth unto the LORD" (Psalm 3:8). He testified, "No more self-made plans. No more sleepless nights, trying to work things out. I eagerly enter into my Shepherd's love. I welcome His open arms toward me, and I am going to lie down in His rest. I am going to sleep peacefully in His unconditional love for me."

Jehovah Rohi Is Your Shepherd, Too

David knew that *Jehovah Rohi* was his Shepherd—and the Lord is also Shepherd over every hurting, despairing sheep who has been wounded by the world. Our great Shepherd loves every sheep who has gone astray because of testing, trials, hurts and wounds. We should never dare to accuse our Shepherd of abandoning us. He still walks beside us and watches over us at all times.

Perhaps right now you are fighting a losing war against some kind of temptation. You may be battling a pornography addiction, homosexuality, alcoholism, adultery, materialism or an unruly tongue. Whatever your struggle is, you have determined not to run away from the Lord. All around you, people try to justify their sin. They look for alibis and make excuses, but you refuse to give yourself over to sin's grasp. Instead, you have taken God's Word to heart.

Yet like David you have grown weary, and now you have come to the point where you feel absolutely helpless. The enemy is pounding you with despair, fear and lies. Perhaps you have entertained thoughts of suicide.

I urge you: Do not give in to despair. Every true follower of Jesus eventually goes through what you are experiencing. It does not matter what your temptation may be; we all face the reality of indwelling sin, and yet we have a Shepherd who loves us and comes after us.

The worst thing you can do right now is to stop turning to the Lord. Do not stop going to His house and having fellowship with other believers. Do not turn to the world's solutions. Jesus tells all of us, "Follow Me." If you will keep acknowledging Him and following Him up the hillside, He will eventually lead you down the other side, to the green valley of healing and restoration.

Keep yourself in a repentant, sin-resistant attitude. Believe that soon you will find yourself in the rest that God's love provides. Your Shepherd knows everything about you, including your darkest places—and He still loves you. He knows where the green pastures are and He is going to lead you to them. He will come after you and call you by name. When you answer, He will assure you, "You have nothing to be depressed about. I am by your side."

Perhaps you are a devoted believer who has known and experienced the deeper things of God. You may be a veteran of intense spiritual warfare. You may have ministered to others mightily in the Lord. You may have received deep revelations of God that others have not. Yet, right now, you are going through a dark night of the soul that no one could ever imagine. Nobody can relate to the awful pain you face every day, the endless anguish you are enduring. Maybe this is by far the most terrible trial you have ever experienced.

Your testing may become even more mystifying and unexplainable, but I want you to know that no matter what you are going through the Holy Spirit wants to reveal to you *Jehovah Rohi*—the Lord, your Shepherd. He wants to imprint His love on your heart. In fact, everything you are going through is meant to bring you into the indescribable confidence that He loves you.

Jesus assured us, "I will never leave you nor forsake you," and our heavenly Father—*Jehovah Rohi,* the Lord our Shepherd—has revealed Himself to us in Psalm 23. He tells us, "I know you by name, and I know what you are going through. Come, lie down in My grace and love. Don't try to figure out everything. Just accept My love for you and rest in my loving arms.

"Yes, I am the Lord of hosts. I am the majestic and holy God. I want you to know all of these revelations about Me, but the one revelation I want you to have right now is the revelation of *Jehovah Rohi*. I want you to know Me as your loving, caring Shepherd, and I want you to rest assured that I will bring you through all your trials, in my tenderness and love."

Our circumstances may not change, but we can trust our Shepherd to lead us into the green valley. It does not matter how awfully our enemies press in on us. The Lord has proven His love to us time after time.

nine

Immanuel

God with Us

As a Christian you have probably heard biblical teaching on the subject of spiritual warfare. Most such teaching centers on Paul's exhortation to the church in Ephesians 6:12: "We wrestle not against flesh and blood, but against principalities, against powers, against the rulers of the darkness of this world, against spiritual wickedness in high places." You may wonder how and when this spiritual warfare began.

We find the origin of all spiritual warfare in Genesis 3. In the Garden of Eden, Satan had just finished tempting Eve. He deceived her into eating the fruit from the forbidden tree, and

160

in that very hour God declared war on the devil. He told Satan in no uncertain terms: "Because thou hast done this . . . I will put enmity between thee and the woman, and between thy seed and her seed; it shall bruise thy head, and thou shalt bruise his heel" (Genesis 3:14–15).

God was putting Satan on notice. As Scripture later showed, He was saying, "You have attempted to destroy My handiwork. I decree, therefore, that one day a Child will come forth from a woman to be My ruler, and this Child will be your enemy. You are going to injure His foot, and you will think you have defeated Him. But afterward, He will plant His foot on your head and crush it. He is going to decimate all your power and authority. He is going to defeat you completely, destroying your kingdom of darkness."

This news must have struck Satan with terror. It probably sent him into a panic: "Will I recognize when this seed arrives? Who will this Child be? Who is going to remove all my power and destroy me? When will He come? How can I expect to know Him?"

Satan is not all-knowing. He could not possibly know whom God was speaking of when He referred to this seed. The devil knew of Christ, of course, before he fell from heaven. Satan was Lucifer then, a part of the heavenly councils of God. So he obviously knew the only begotten Son of the Father. But once the devil was cast out of heaven he was no longer privy to God's plans. He knew nothing of the incarnation that was to come. Now, as the Lord declared war, Satan had no way of knowing exactly what was going to happen. He did not know who the coming Child would be, who His mother would be or when she would deliver Him.

Satan probably trembled when Eve gave birth to Cain, her firstborn. Eve must have believed Cain was the promised seed, because she announced, "I have gotten a man from the LORD" (Genesis 4:1). In turn, the devil must have wondered, *Could* this be the promised Child, the seed who is coming as my destroyer? I can imagine the relief he felt when Cain slew his brother, Abel. Satan probably thought, *This man could not possibly be the holy seed. He doesn't show the character of heaven, because he has committed an evil act.*

Satan must have felt the same panic every time a righteous man came on the scene. I wonder, what did he think when godly Enoch appeared, someone who was said to walk with God? Enoch lived for 365 years, preaching righteousness all of his days. The devil must have lived in fear with every passing year of this godly man's life wondering if Enoch was his destroyer. Satan probably thought the same of righteous Noah who Scripture says found grace in the Lord's eyes.

No doubt Satan was relieved when Enoch suddenly disappeared, taken up to heaven by the Lord Himself. This man was not the incarnate seed. Likewise the devil was probably relieved when he saw Noah get drunk. In both cases Satan could breathe a sigh of relief.

Then Abraham came on the scene. I picture Satan quaking in terror this time. Abraham was the son of an idol worshiper, but something was obviously special about this man. When God instructed him to pull up stakes and travel to a far country, Abraham obeyed immediately. Later, when Abraham came to Bethel, he built an altar to the Lord. After that Satan probably kept a close watch on Abraham's movements, eyeing his every step.

The devil might have gloated when Abraham's wife, Sarah, was taken into Pharaoh's harem. Satan probably hoped, *Surely this isn't the woman who will give birth to the righteous seed. Pharaoh will most likely impregnate her, and she'll give birth to a heathen son. No such child could be the holy one.* Satan also probably did his best to see that Sarah was defiled in the harem but God protected her supernaturally.

The devil might have been temporarily relieved when he heard Abraham telling half-truths to protect himself. Satan had

---

Knowing God by Name

to be further relieved when Abraham's concubine gave birth to Ishmael. Now the devil probably thought, *I know for a fact this cannot be the holy seed. He has been born of a concubine.* Ishmael's name means "God will hear"—but he still was not the seed.

Satan saw Isaac and many other righteous men come and go over the years. Finally, Moses prophesied that a man would come in the last days who would be like himself. (By this Moses meant that he himself was only a type, a foreshadowing, of the Messiah.) At that point Satan knew his destroyer's arrival was marked for a date further into the future. As each of the prophets spoke of the coming Messiah, the devil took note of their words.

It Is Not Our Fight

Let me remind you here of a principle we learned earlier. Our spiritual warfare has never been about human life. It has always been a war between our heavenly Father and the devil. Ever since God declared war on Satan, prophesying that the holy seed was coming to destroy him, the devil has waged war to try to destroy that seed.

I think I know the moment when Satan got his first hint about where the seed would come from. In Genesis 17 God promised to give Abraham a seed in his old age and to multiply that seed. I believe Satan overheard this conversation. He paid attention when God made a covenant with Abraham and his seed, saying, "I'm going to give you a son, Abraham, and I'm going to make an everlasting covenant with your son. I promise that this son will be the father of many nations."

God also said to Sarah, "I will establish My covenant between Me and thee and thy seed after thee in their generations for an everlasting covenant, to be a God unto thee, and to thy seed after thee" (Genesis 17:7).

Isaac, Abraham's son, would not be the prophesied seed. But the seed—Satan's destroyer—would come through Isaac's seed, from the seed of Abraham. We are aware that the devil knows the Scriptures. He twisted them as he quoted them to Jesus, tempting the Lord in the wilderness. So surely the enemy knew from Old Testament prophecies that the Messiah would come to earth by way of a woman's womb. He knew that eventually this Messiah would rise up to save humankind and crush his power. But the question remained: Which woman would the Child come from, and where and when would He come?

The devil learned some more clues when he heard God's promises to David. As Nathan prophesied to David, suddenly the picture became clear:

> Go and tell my servant David . . . the LORD telleth thee that he will make thee an house. . . . I will set up thy seed after thee, which shall proceed out of thy bowels, and I will establish his kingdom. He shall build an house for my name, and I will establish the throne of his kingdom forever. I will be his father, and he shall be my son.
>
> 2 Samuel 7:5, 11–14

Without question, Nathan was prophesying that God would send His own Son, Jesus, to set up His eternal Kingdom, and this Son would be the seed of Abraham, the lion of the tribe of Judah.

Now some believe that Nathan was referring to Solomon, David's literal son. After all, Solomon built God's house by constructing the Temple in Jerusalem. But the Temple Solomon built lasted only a few hundred years; eventually, it was torn down by God Himself and cast aside as an abomination. According to Nathan's prophecy, the house that God's seed would establish would last forever. Thus, it is clear that the Temple Nathan refers to is the Body of Jesus Christ, His Church.

Another reason that some teachers believe this passage refers only to Solomon is the next sentence. The King James Version says of the seed, "If he commit iniquity, I will chasten him with the rod of men" (7:14). This phrasing, however, is not the proper translation of the verse. Helen Spurrell's original Hebrew translation reads, "Even in his suffering for iniquity, I will chasten him with the rod of men, and with the stripes of the children of men." This echoes the passage in Hebrews that says we are healed by Jesus' stripes—stripes of suffering inflicted by the rod of men.

After Nathan's prophecy, the devil probably figured he was getting closer to uncovering the identity of the seed. Since the chosen Child, God's Son, would reign as a lion out of Judah, Satan turned his focus to that region and tribe. I believe this is the reason why so many mighty empires and armies marched against this tiny nation throughout history.

Think about it: Judah was a non-strategic, arid country filled primarily with poor shepherds and a lot of livestock. There were no ores or precious metals in the hills. At one time it had been a land of milk and honey, but by this time Judah had been struck by severe famines and almost been destroyed in war. So why would great kingdoms like Egypt, Babylon and Assyria attack this insignificant nation?

The answer seems simple to me: The devil was waging these wars. He wanted to kill the seed, to drive it from the face of the earth before it could destroy him. Satan himself was behind these pagan kings, possessing them, driving them, directing them to go after tiny Judah. Satan's one goal was to enter into this small nation and ruin it completely. He wanted to kill Judah's king and set up his own ruler so that he could inhabit a human pawn, ruling over the tribe to monitor its every movement.

Rezin, Pekah and Satan

The seventh chapter of Isaiah reveals one of Satan's most overt attempts to implement his evil plot against Judah. In one hellish swoop, the devil tried to invade Jerusalem, destroy Judah's king and set up his own man on the throne. This chapter describes a very real war, but it also reveals a powerful foreshadowing of the spiritual warfare we face today.

Satan prompted two evil kings to attack Judah. These two kings were named Rezin and Pekah, pagan men who "went up toward Jerusalem to war against it" (Isaiah 7:1). We see Satan's designs against Judah in the pact these two men made together. Rezin and Pekah determined to join forces to "go up against Judah, and vex it, and let us make a breach therein for us, and set a king in the midst of it, even the son of Tabeal" (7:6).

Judah's king at the time was Ahaz, an evil man. Satan was terrified of Ahaz just the same, because he was from David's lineage. The devil decided that this man had to be slain; otherwise, his lineage would produce the destroying seed to come. So Satan went on the attack. He was convinced that he could use Rezin and Pekah to march into Jerusalem, take Ahaz captive and put his own king on Judah's throne.

We know that Jerusalem, God's holy city, is a representation of the Church. It represents the Kingdom of God in our hearts where King Jesus sits enthroned, ruling and reigning in us. In this scene in Isaiah 7 we are seeing a picture of satanic attack on the enthroned Christ in our hearts.

Under the devil's direction, Rezin and Pekah mounted a massive, overwhelming attack against Judah. They quickly overtook a nearby city called Elath. Then the two kings spread their armies out over the land, overflowing the nation's cities. By chapter 7, they had already taken a major portion of Judah.

If you doubt that this was a well-planned, Satan-directed war, consider the Hebrew names of the two kings. The name *Rezin* means "to open the eyes, the senses." And *Pekah* means "good, pleasurable." Where have we read these terms together before? We recognize them from the Garden of Eden, where Satan tempted Eve: "The tree was good . . . pleasant to the eyes, and a tree to be desired to make one wise . . . and the eyes of them both were opened" (Genesis 3:6–7). Undoubtedly, Rezin

---

Knowing God by Name

and Pekah represent the powers of darkness, descending on Jerusalem to destroy it.

Now at first glance it appears that God Himself directed the two pagan kings' attack against Judah. Scripture says, "The LORD began to send against Judah Rezin the king of Syria, and Pekah" (2 Kings 15:37). This verse does not mean, however, that God literally directed these evil men. It simply means that He did not stop Satan in his plans. Make no mistake, the Lord knew exactly what the devil had in mind. But He also knew that Satan's scheme was going to be in vain.

Satan wanted to destroy not only Ahaz, but also the women and children of Judah. He wanted to wipe out even the slightest chance that the seed of Abraham might come to power. In addition, the man whom Satan intended to put on King David's throne was called "the son of Tabeal." In Hebrew, this name means "almighty idol, deity."

After most of Judah had been taken, Rezin and Pekah met outside Jerusalem, regrouping in order to launch a massive onslaught against the city of God. Jerusalem's leaders trembled when they heard that a great, confederated army was poised to wage war against them: "[Ahaz's] heart was moved, and the heart of his people, as the trees of the wood are moved with the wind" (Isaiah 7:2). Everyone wondered, "Who will protect the house of David? What will happen to the promises God made to our former king? Is the seed in danger?"

God had already made an ironclad promise to His servant David: "The LORD hath sworn in truth unto David; he will not turn from it; of the fruit of thy body will I set upon thy throne" (Psalm 132:11). The Lord was telling David, "There will always be one of your seed, one of your sons, on the throne." It is clear to us today that God was speaking of the Kingdom to come through Jesus. Christ Himself, the seed of David, would occupy that throne.

But now the house of David was in total panic, God's Spirit came upon Isaiah to bring forth a word to King Ahaz. The Lord told Isaiah, "Go to Ahaz at the upper gate. You will find him inspecting the city's water supply. I want you to give him this message: 'Ahaz, you see the armies coming upon you. They have a plan to set up their own king in the midst of Jerusalem. But you are not to panic. The Lord says: Their schemes will never come to pass.'"

> Take heed and be quiet; fear not, neither be fainthearted for the two tails of these smoking firebrands, for the fierce anger of Rezin with Syria, and of the son of Remaliah. Because Syria, Ephraim, and the son of Remaliah, have taken evil counsel against thee, saying, Let us go up against Judah, and vex it, and let us make a breach therein for us, and set a king in the midst of it, even the son of Tabeal: Thus saith the Lord GOD, It shall not stand, neither shall it come to pass.
>
> Isaiah 7:4–7

Isaiah found Ahaz just where the Lord had told him. The king was inspecting the water conduit outside Jerusalem's walls to make sure nothing disturbed the city's drinking supply when the enemy arrived. Here we see a picture of a man trusting totally in his flesh. Ahaz had already sent a delegation to Assyria's king to try to hire his army to save Jerusalem. Ahaz had paid a price, in silver and gold, to try to obtain a defense against the two kings.

Was God's promise to David truly in jeopardy? Was the lion of the tribe of Judah actually in danger? Not according to what God had prophesied to Isaiah. The Lord explained, "These two kings are like firebrands. They may look fierce, red-hot and flaming, but I have totally taken the fire out of them. Now they are nothing but smoke. Their plan against you isn't going to work, Ahaz. Just be quiet, be still and trust in Me."

Shadow and Flame

Isaiah told Ahaz that he had nothing to fear: "As for King Rezin, his power is in its death throes. Within sixty-five years there won't even be a nation left of his people. They are going to be wiped off the face of the earth. I'm telling you, Ahaz, these kings are nothing but smoke. The Lord has put out their fire. They are powerless. Don't you understand? These men are not your true enemy. God sent me here to tell you this is not the real war. It's just a skirmish. The real war is farther along, way down the line. God says this battle in front of you is already over, finished. So you have nothing to fear. Your throne will continue if you will just believe that God will sustain it."

Isaiah then gave Ahaz a clear warning from the Lord: "If ye will not believe, surely ye shall not be established" (Isaiah 7:9). The prophet explained to the faithless king, "The house of David and his seed are going to be established by faith alone. You have to believe God will be true to His covenant oath."

Isaiah knew that throughout the whole war Ahaz had been trusting in the flesh. He was fully aware that the king had relied on his armies and on his own skill and wit in putting together a deal with Assyria.

Here we see two distinct ways in which God's people believe they will be delivered from Satan and his snares. First, there is the way Isaiah exhorted Ahaz: "Believe, and surely you will be established." This is the way of faith, the way of trusting fully in the covenant promises of God. But there is also the way Ahaz went at first—turning to the power of flesh. This is the way of human ability—of calling upon "King Willpower" to come and save us rather than our true deliverer, King Jesus.

Maybe Satan's principalities have brought such an intense spiritual warfare upon you that you have become ensnared by a sinful habit. No matter how hard you have prayed you have not been able to find victory. So now you are sending your flesh out to do battle with the enemy. You are trying to force a change by relying on your own human strength.

It will never work. Why? Because God is not interested in giving you victory over a single sin. The Lord is after more in your life than merely one bad habit. This is not just a one-time battle; God sees the ongoing spiritual warfare your enemy constantly brings against you. He wants to give you a victory that will establish you for the long term. He wants you to be able to say more than, "I once had this sin in my life but now I've overcome it." Instead He wants you to be so totally established in your faith that absolutely nothing can destroy Christ's rule in your heart. That way, when the enemy comes against you smoking like the fires from hell, you will not have to waver like a tree in the wind.

This is just what God wanted to do for King Ahaz and the nation of Judah. Even though Ahaz was a wicked king and the people were disobedient and half-asleep in their faith, God still protected them. The reason God kept pressing Ahaz was because He still loved him. Though this sensual king was far from the Lord, God would not relent in trying to persuade him to turn aside from his ways of flesh and put his trust in God.

A Sign from Heaven

The Lord urged Ahaz, "Ask thee a sign of the LORD thy God; ask it either in the depth, or in the height above" (Isaiah 7:11). The Lord was extending an incredible invitation to Judah's wicked king. He was saying to Ahaz, "Your faith is weak so I want you to ask Me for a sign—any sign, miracle or wonder, from heaven down to hell. I want to do a wondrous work for you to birth true faith in your heart."

You may be shocked that God would make such an offer to any human. Didn't Jesus say only an evil generation seeks after a sign? Didn't He say there was just one sign—Himself? Yes,

Jesus did say that, and I believe that Christ was the very sign God wanted to show Ahaz. The Lord wanted to reveal His saving, delivering power through a miraculous work of His own faithfulness. Indeed, as we look closer, we see that this passage is all about Jesus.

But Ahaz refused to ask God for such a work. Why? He had already committed to trusting in his own wisdom, and he tried to disguise his fleshly decision as one of godliness. "Ahaz said, I will not ask, neither will I tempt the LORD" (Isaiah 7:12). The wicked king was saying, "I refuse to tempt God. I would never ask Him for a supernatural sign. That wouldn't be holy." Ahaz had put on a robe of self-righteousness.

How did the Lord answer Ahaz? He told him, "Therefore the LORD Himself shall give you a sign" (Isaiah 7:14). God said, "So, you won't ask for a sign? Well, I'm going to give you one anyway." Here was the sign from the Lord: "Behold, a virgin shall conceive, and bear a son, and shall call his name Immanuel" (verse 14). The name *Immanuel* means "God with us."

It was obvious to both Isaiah and Ahaz that this prophecy had nothing to do with Judah's present battle. The word God delivered here was about an event that would be fulfilled sometime in the future. Ahaz must have been baffled by this. Why would the Lord give him a sign that apparently had nothing to do with the war before him? He probably complained to Isaiah, "You're prophesying of a deliverer who might not come for years. What about this present war, our present danger? What possible good could this prophecy be to us right now?"

I believe God's purpose in speaking this word to Ahaz was simple. He was assuring the sin-blinded king that if Jerusalem still existed in the future, then the battle before him now could not be the end of Judah. God was giving His people then—as well as His Church today—a very clear message:

"Is your faith so weak that you cannot believe Me for this present battle? I am going to tell you something that will build up your faith for every battle, now and in the future. There is coming to earth an *Immanuel*, 'God with us.' Why do I tell you this? I want you to know that Judah will still be standing in the future. If I have promised that your nation will still be here when *Immanuel* arrives years from now, then you do not need to worry about this present battle. You are safe, Ahaz. I am telling you: In the future *Immanuel* is going to sit on the throne you are sitting on now, ruling and reigning. This is the throne of David. And I am not going to allow anyone to harm it.

"Therefore, Ahaz, the battle you see before you is not the real battle. It is just a minor skirmish. Satan will never prevail over Judah. He is not going to set up his throne in Jerusalem. I simply won't allow it. So I have already declared this war to be over before it has even begun."

And so it was. God blew away those two approaching powers. His message through it all was simple: "If you will trust Me, you will never be in any danger. I am going to make sure the throne is established. Lean on Me, instead of on the strength of your flesh."

A War to End All Wars

In the days of Isaiah the final war was still a long way off, not to begin until the prophesied virgin gave birth to a son whose name was *Immanuel*.

Matthew echoes Isaiah's prophecy of *Immanuel*, the Child to come: "Behold, a virgin shall be with child, and shall bring forth a son, and they shall call his name Emmanuel, which being interpreted is, God with us" (Matthew 1:23). This passage also names the child: "She shall bring forth a son, and thou shalt call his name JESUS: for he shall save his people from their sins" (verse 21). Immanuel's name is Jesus, meaning in full, "Jesus is God with us."

Knowing God by Name

When that seed, the Christ, arrived, there was no mistaking the event. Satan could not possibly have missed the time, place or arrival of the promised Child, Jesus. There could be no question about it because it was announced from the very heavens. Angels proclaimed it from the skies: "He has come!" Wise men came from afar to see Him. Shepherds gathered from the hills to worship Him—and He was named *Immanuel.*

At this point Satan knew his warfare was no longer just a skirmish. Now he knew exactly who the chosen Child was: Jesus. Yet God protected the Christ Child from the enemy. He hid him away in Egypt, where Satan did not know His whereabouts. I remind you, the devil is not omniscient. The only thing he knew was what was revealed in Scripture, that the promised Child would come out of Bethlehem.

After Christ arrived, Satan used Herod to slaughter every male baby in the area, hoping that the promised Child was among them. The devil then spent 33 years trying to kill Jesus. When the Lord was about to begin His public ministry, Satan tried to destroy Him by urging Him to leap from the roof of the Temple. Throughout His life, our Lord was faced continually with the enemy's attempts to kill Him.

Finally, at the cross, the powers of hell thought their hour of triumph had come. When Jesus was killed, all of hell must have had a celebration. Satan and his demonic powers were probably convinced, "He's dead now. We've finally killed Him! That's it, the end of the battle! So much for the seed. We've won!" But three days later, hallelujah! Jesus rose from the grave; the seed was alive and well.

What a surprise *that* must have been to Satan! Just as God foretold in the Garden of Eden, the devil had only succeeded in bruising Jesus' heel. The poison had not worked after all, and now the seed had returned, His heel utterly crushing Satan's power. King Jesus was now on the throne. Christ, the seed of David, had defeated Satan once and for all, vanquishing his principalities and powers, and today we look forward to the day when God will cast the enemy into a lake of fire for good, to be tormented forever.

How Does This Affect Us Today?

Christ is in glory, safely removed from all harm, yet we are still here on earth, engaged in spiritual warfare with the devil and his principalities and powers. What does it mean, exactly, that Jesus has defeated Satan and given us the victory?

When we talk about the devil being defeated, we are referring to his goal of destroying the seed. The enemy cannot touch Jesus now because Christ sits at the right hand of the Father in glory, beyond Satan's reach. That battle is over, finished. The enemy can never reach his ultimate goal of destroying Christ, the seed. All the prophecies from throughout the centuries have been fulfilled, and Satan has lost the war. In this sense, Jesus has taken away all of the devil's power.

We also are the seed of God, however. Everyone who has enthroned Jesus as Lord and Savior in his heart and mind is Christ's own Body—still here on earth. When Jesus ascended to glory, Satan declared war on His earthly seed. So the enemy is waging war once again; only now the battle is for the hearts of God's people. The devil's strategy has not changed. He is still attempting to march into the New Jerusalem—that is, into our hearts—to unseat Christ and enthrone himself as ruler over our lives.

The book of Revelation tells us that Satan sent a flood after the people of Judah (represented as a pregnant woman, because they gave birth to Jesus) in order to destroy them. We see the same thing happening all around us today. A flood of iniquity has been poured out on the earth in an effort to destroy the seed. Make no mistake: Hellish principalities are still waging war. The Pekahs and Rezins we face today have but one goal and one desire: to kill the Church, Christ's beloved Bride. Their intent is this: "I am going to destroy Christ's Body here on earth, one by one. I am going to poison His heel and bruise it."

Nowhere to Hide

Have you crowned Jesus as Lord and King of your body, soul and spirit? Does Jesus sit on the throne of your heart? Does He rule your life as head, directing your every action and decision? If so, the hordes of hell have marked you as a target for warfare. As surely as Satan came against Judah, he will also come against you. He will throw at you all the weapons in his arsenal—temptations, trials, despair, discouragement. He will attack you for one reason: He wants to weaken your faith and trust in *Immanuel*. His goal is to get you to drift away from the Lordship of Christ.

Right now you may find yourself standing in satanic floodwaters up to your neck. Maybe you have been flailing frantically, doing your best just to keep from drowning, but afraid you soon may go under. That is exactly what happened to Judah in the book of Isaiah. Here is what the prophet cried out:

> Now, therefore, behold, the Lord bringeth up upon them the waters of the river, strong and many, even the king of Assyria, and all his glory: and he shall come up over all his channels, and go over all his banks: and he shall pass through Judah; he shall overflow and go over, he shall reach even to the neck; and the stretching out of his wings shall fill the breadth of thy land, O Immanuel.
>
> Isaiah 8:7–8

Consider how the Lord answered Judah's enemies: "Give ear, all ye of far countries: gird yourselves, and ye shall be broken in pieces; gird yourselves, and ye shall be broken in pieces" (Isaiah 8:9). Isaiah proclaimed, "Take counsel together, and it shall come to nought; speak the word, and it shall not stand: for God is with us" (verse 10).

Isaiah's bold words apply just as well to the Church of Jesus Christ today. The prophet is telling us, "Let Satan and all his demonic forces make their plans. Let them hold meetings and consultations. All their plots and schemes are going to fail. They can never overthrow Christ from the throne of His Church."

I believe that the enemy sends certain messengers from hell to buffet us. This was true in both the Old and New Testaments. The Old Testament identifies the king of Persia as a spiritual entity—a demonic force who withstood the angel Gabriel, causing a battle that lasted for days. Likewise in the New Testament, Paul speaks of evil intelligence in the spiritual realm that do battle against us.

I imagine the devil and his cohorts holding hellish counsels to plot their warfare against us. This evil empire is made up of captains, authorities, masters of many kinds of demonic devices—all under Satan's direction. They put their heads together to strategize their attacks, aiming especially at anointed servants who have subjected their lives totally to Jesus' Lordship. They are determined to bring down every godly preacher of the Gospel, every lay worker, every sincere believer who has enthroned Christ in his heart. If you are such a servant, you can know a hellish strategy is being formed against you right now inside the gates of hell.

I believe that once these evil spirits agree on their plans, they rise up and arm themselves with demonic weapons. They fill their quivers with poison arrows laced with malice, hatred and gossip. Then they draw their swords and sharpen them with anger, revenge and murder. They dip their knives into the poison of despair, confusion and discouragement. Finally, Satan sends them off on their assignments to make war against the seed of God.

I picture these evil warriors going forth full of pride and arrogance, confident that they are going to bring down the Kingdom of God. Their war cry is, "Destroy the seed, take the throne." They are determined to march straight into the holy Jerusalem of your heart, topple King Jesus from His reign there and prepare the throne for Satan to be set upon it.

There is no doubt that these evil powers are assigned to individual believers' lives. The New Testament tells us that one such power was assigned to Paul. I believe the same is true for every Christian today. The devil sends forth numerous evil spirits from his war council, instructing them to tempt and trouble us, to flood our hearts with loneliness, guilt and despair.

I imagine, for example, Satan sending one of his fiercest captains to torment a dear elderly sister in Christ I know. This woman is a 92-year-old prayer warrior who attends our church. She is not well known in our congregation, but she is feared in hell because she lives only to please Jesus. I am sure the demonic entity assigned to her has been told, "She's your assignment. Now, go and dispatch her."

Even as we consider hell's war councils against us, we have to remember what Isaiah prophesied: "The enemy shall be broken and his weapons destroyed. The Lord will smash him into pieces. All of his counsel, plans and assignments will fail. Jesus Christ shall never be dethroned. If you will simply believe, you shall be established." (See Isaiah 7:4–7.)

Christ, Our Protector and Strength

I would love to look in on those war councils when hell's warriors return from their assignments. After waging war, these demonic principalities must have to report to the devil, and as they return, I am sure there is no more war cry, no more enthusiasm, no more pride or arrogance. Instead, these warriors walk into the council room with their heads hanging.

They have been beaten, scarred, crushed, and they are licking their wounds. Their weapons have been taken from them, broken and obliterated. All their plots have been brought to nothing.

The entity assigned to the elderly woman of prayer whimpers, "I thought she would be an easy assignment. So I nicked her with a poisoned arrow of fear. I whispered that she was going to die soon. I saw the effects of my attack immediately as she was discouraged for hours. She doubted that God was going to take care of her. I thought she was finished! I was convinced that I'd gotten through.

"But then that little old woman got on her knees. She cried out, '*Immanuel*, please help me. Come and deliver me.' And suddenly, *He* appeared. He touched the poisoned spot where I had nicked her, and in the blink of an eye she was healed. Then He grabbed my quiver of poisoned arrows and emptied it. He broke all the arrows and tossed them aside like toothpicks. Then He looked me in the eye—and the next thing I knew, I was on the ground with His foot on my neck. He rubbed my face in the ground and sent me fleeing.

"Before I left, He gave me a message for you, Satan. He said, 'Take heed—*Immanuel* lives here. Put your warriors on notice. This woman is not alone. If you come around here again, you will have to deal with *Immanuel*, God with her.'"

Another entity raises its head and laments, "I was the messenger assigned to buffet the apostle Paul. I did everything I could to that man to try to bring him down. I tell you, nothing worked!

"I beat Paul, shipwrecked him, threw him into the ocean and then slandered him. I turned the whole world against him. I pulled out every weapon in my arsenal—used everything on the list and then invented a few! At one point I thought I'd killed him, but as I turned to walk away, I heard him preaching louder than ever!

"So I had him thrown into prison. But while Paul was praying and worshiping in chains, the *Immanuel* Christ appeared. He unlocked Paul's bonds, opened the prison doors and sent the apostle out preaching, stronger still. Then *Immanuel* picked me up and cast me out. He told me that everything I did to Paul was in vain, that I was only making him a stronger warrior!

"Please, I can't go back on assignment against Paul. Every time I try to follow the apostle, I see *Immanuel* with him. The more I attack him, the more he turns to Jesus. I beg you, Satan, send someone else."

You will never be aware of all the times an evil entity has been assigned to attack you. Those hellish principalities are bent on tempting you, trying you beyond your limits, destroying your faith. But, unbeknownst to you, every one of those spirits has been sent back to the kingdom of darkness defeated, injured and shamed. *Immanuel* withstood them, and all you had to do was trust in Him. You believed God would fight your battle, and He did it. He drove them all away.

Now all of hell knows that Jesus is on the throne of your heart. The devil has been soundly defeated; he knows he cannot touch Christ's throne in you, and every power in hell is aware that *Immanuel* is with you.

If Immanuel Is with You, Who Can Harm You?

Picture a Christian man who has been delivered from pornography. He has enjoyed a year or so of consistent victory over his former habit. Then one day he walks by a video store and sees tapes in the window that stir up his old lusts. The demonic entity assigned to him is aware of his old weakness, and now he comes against that saint with every weapon in his arsenal. He lures the man toward an X-rated video, and the man picks it up and takes it home.

Imagine the report this evil messenger brings back to Satan. He tells the adversary, "For half an hour this man feasted his eyes on the pornography in his video player. His old lusts were inflamed. But then, out of nowhere, he began crying out, 'Oh, Jesus, help me!'—and that's when it happened!

"Suddenly the man leaped out of his chair, ejected the tape and tore the ribbon out with his bare hands! Then he walked through his apartment shouting, 'I'm free, I'm free!'

"I thought I had him, Satan! I thought he was finished, but *Immanuel* showed up when he called, and I was tossed out on my head! God was with this man."

The truth is, God never forsook that man for a single moment. *Immanuel,* King Jesus, was with him the whole time. He was with him in the video store, on the way home and in his living room when he watched the video. Faithful as only He can be, Jesus intervened as soon as His broken servant cried out, "Help me, Lord!"

This is to be our victorious confession: "*Immanuel* is with me at all times, in my every waking and sleeping hour. God made an oath to me. He said that if I believed *Immanuel,* I would be established, immovable, impregnable, and I believe He is with me—abiding in me, walking alongside me, protecting me. If God is with me, therefore, who can be against me?"

That is God's desire—to have a people who will trust Him with all their trials, temptations and victories. He wants them to be totally established by their faith in Him. Even wicked Ahaz and the people of Judah were delivered and rescued from their war. Because they trusted in their own flesh, they were eventually disciplined. (Remember, it is not enough to win just one battle against hell's powers.) Yet, by grace alone, God faithfully preserved the Davidic throne of wicked Ahaz. He even preserved backslidden Judah because He had made a covenant with their fathers.

Will not the Lord also preserve the throne He has set up in the hearts of His righteous people? Will not He also keep His covenant oath with those who love and trust in Him? We alone can cast Jesus from the throne of our hearts by willfully turning from Him.

We are to trust in *Immanuel,* "God with us." No matter what temptation, trial or fiery weapon from hell you may face, you can rest assured in His faithful hands. He has made an oath to His people. He will be faithful to keep it.

ten

His Name Is *Forgiveness*

The God Who Pardons

How is our Lord distinguished from all the other gods worshiped throughout the world? We know, of course, that our God is above all others, set apart in every way, but one characteristic that distinguishes Him from every other god is this: He is *the God who pardons*.

Scripture reveals our Lord as the God who forgives, the only God who has the power to pardon sin:

> Who is a God like unto thee, that pardoneth iniquity, and passeth by the transgression of the remnant of his heritage? He retaineth

not his anger for ever, because he delighteth in mercy. He will turn again, he will have compassion upon us; he will subdue our iniquities; and thou wilt cast all their sins into the depths of the sea.

Micah 7:18–19

Many other witnesses confirmed this. Look at the words of Nehemiah, Moses and David.

Nehemiah declared, "Thou art a God ready to pardon, gracious and merciful, slow to anger, and of great kindness, and forsookest them not" (Nehemiah 9:17). The proper translation of the phrase *a God ready to pardon* is "a God of propitiation" or "a God of forgiveness."

The people Nehemiah was referring to were the disobedient Israelites. The Lord did not forsake His people even when they rebelled against His Word. Instead He said by His actions, "My people were disobedient, but My nature is to pardon. Forgiving is not just something I do—it is who I am. I am merciful, a God who pardons. I will not turn My back on My people."

On Mount Sinai, Moses asked the Lord for a revelation of His glory. He was not allowed to see God's face, but the Lord did reveal Himself to Moses through a proclamation of His name. Scripture says, "The LORD descended in the cloud, and stood with him there, and proclaimed the name of the LORD" (Exodus 34:5).

What name did God reveal to Moses? It was this: "The LORD God, merciful and gracious, longsuffering, and abundant in goodness and truth, keeping mercy for thousands, forgiving iniquity and transgression and sin" (verses 6–7).

Here was the name that God wanted His children to know Him by. The Lord was saying, "If you want to know who I am, and what I am all about, this is it. Here is My glory—that I forgive all sin, iniquity and transgression. You ask for a revelation of My nature? Here is how I want you to know Me."

David gave us the same Hebrew description of God. He wrote, "For thou, LORD, art good, and ready to forgive; and plenteous in mercy unto all them that call upon thee" (Psalm 86:5). David called God good, ready to forgive and overflowing with mercy. Remember, he penned these words out of his own difficult personal experience!

After sinning against the Lord, David sank into a deep depression. He was gripped with terror because of his iniquity. He spent many days when he actually despaired of life. In the Psalms he described the experience as being "in the depths." Finally, out of this despair, David cried to the Lord: "Out of the depths have I cried unto thee, O LORD. . . . If thou, LORD, shouldest mark iniquities, O LORD, who shall stand?" (Psalm 130:1, 3).

Through the testimony of these men—Nehemiah, Moses and David—we see three confirming revelations of the forgiving nature of our God. Nehemiah proclaimed the Lord's forgiveness through a prophetic revelation. Moses described it through a revelation given by the Lord Himself. David wrote of God's mercy and forgiveness through his own personal experience with it.

The Comfort of God's Pardon

Let's look for a moment at the revelation given to David. David was like many Christians today. He was a faithful, devoted believer. He served the Lord gladly. But at one point he fell into grievous sin. Afterward he had a sense that God was marking down his iniquities. To *mark iniquities* means to hold or reserve our failures so that eventually we have to face God's wrath and punishment for them. David could not escape the nagging feeling that the Lord was keeping a close record of each one of his transgressions.

David knew that he would never survive such judgment. He cried, in essence, "God, if You are going to judge me by the law, I don't stand a chance. I have failed on every point of it. If You are keeping a record of my failures—stockpiling them so I have to face them at the judgment—I will never make it. I have no hope. I'm already condemned. If You mark our iniquities, Lord, who can stand? Who can be saved, since we all have sinned? All of us are condemned."

Suddenly the Holy Ghost brought David out of the depths of his despair. How did He do this? He gave David a revelation of who God is. David declared triumphantly, "But there is forgiveness with thee, that thou mayest be feared" (Psalm 130: 4). David had been delivered from his terror by a revelation of God's name: "Our Lord forgives. His name is *forgiveness.*" In that moment, David's despair was lifted.

Where had David's despair come from? It came from the thought that God was mad at him. He was convinced that the Lord was against him because he had failed, sinned and committed grievous acts. But the revelation God gave David was, "You will find forgiveness with Me, so that I may be feared."

What does this last phrase, *that thou mayest be feared* (verse 4), mean? Simply this: The fear of God does not come from thinking that there are swords hanging over our heads waiting to crush us when we stumble or fall. True fear of God comes from knowing that we can serve Him in peace because our sins have been blotted out. It is to revere Him for His loving kindness and readiness to forgive.

David was saying, "Lord, I was ready to faint because of my sins. I was on the brink of giving up, but You revealed Your forgiving love to me. Before, I thought You were marking my sins. Now, all I can see is You forgiving my sins and blotting them out. Finally I can go back to worshiping You. I can serve You again. I can obey You with honor and godly fear."

Discovering the Lord as a God who forgives is the only way out of the despair that is brought on by guilt and condemnation. Here is the key to obtaining relief: We are to believe with all our beings that our Lord is a God who forgives our sins. Indeed, this is the only power that can quiet a guilty, accusing conscience.

Most Christians are persuaded that they know all about God's forgiveness, yet too few believers live in the power and enjoyment of this amazing gift. They may know about forgiveness doctrinally and be able to quote all the major passages concerning it, but they do not enjoy God's forgiveness as an ongoing, daily part of their Christian walks. Why?

In spite of all we have been taught about God's mercy—about the victory of the cross, being ransomed by Christ's blood and being freely accepted by grace alone—most of us still live with uncertainty. Many believers have a nagging sense of God's displeasure. Their consciences are in constant turmoil. They are able to teach about God's grace, preach about God's grace and sing about God's grace, but they never fully enjoy it. What they see in the Bible about the Lord's forgiveness simply is not realized in their hearts.

Such Christians have not entered into what Paul calls the "blessedness" of knowing that your sins are not imputed against you (see Galatians 4:15). How does this blessedness manifest itself? It comes as a peace that settles our souls because we know that we have nothing to fear on Judgment Day. No matter how we may feel, or what lies the devil may throw at us, we are confident that there is nothing in God's books against us.

I ask you, when the enemy comes at you with lies, filling you with fear and driving you to despair, what do you do? How are you able to combat him? I can assure you, the only way to deal with guilt and condemnation is to be armed with a true biblical understanding of forgiveness. This kind of understanding is especially needed in these last days as Satan's temptations become even heavier. I believe our generation is going to experience attacks from hell that are more powerful and intense than at any other time in history. These temptations will only get worse, but God's grace and forgiveness is more than equal.

Why do many Christians never enjoy the peace and rest found in forgiveness? Why have they never laid hold of that "blessedness" Paul refers to? Why do they continue to strive, always filled with fear and condemnation? Why can they never seem to escape their depression and despair?

It is because their consciences are thundering inside them. Every time they sin, they come under a cloud of fear that thunders the law at them. Whenever we fail God's law, our consciences pronounce wrath and anger upon our souls. That is their purpose. If you have seared your conscience it will excuse you, but the conscience of a spiritual person will do what God Himself designed it to do. Its voice will not let up: "You have sinned—you are guilty. Now you must be judged! You have to pay the penalty for your sin."

The conscience has two mandates from God: to condemn both sin and the sinner. Here is how I see the conscience having dominion over these two territories.

First, the Lord has entrusted the conscience to condemn sin. The conscience is faithful to expose to us the deceitfulness of sin. It shows us how vile sin is, and it rightly shows us that God cannot abide sin—any sin. It sees what the mirror of the law shows.

Second, God has entrusted the conscience to condemn the one who sins. If you have sinned—disobeyed God's law and broken His commandments—your conscience brings condemnation on you. It informs you that there will be a time when you must give an account.

This is why we feel condemned when we sin: Our consciences condemn us on every point where we break God's law. The conscience knows nothing of forgiveness. It has not been mandated to do that work in our lives. If you could ask your conscience to tell you about forgiveness, it would answer, "That's not my job. God has instructed me to expose to you the wickedness of your sin and to condemn you for committing it. That's all. My job is to come when you sin and disturb your peace. I am supposed to tell you that what you have done is grievous and will ruin you. I am to remind you constantly that God hates sin and that

He is going to judge it. My job is to show you that you won't get away with your sin. God sees everything that you do in secret, and He will make you give an account for it."

The conscience will not move to the left or right on any point of the law. It tells us the truth about God's commandments: "Do this and live. If you fail, you will die." In this sense, the conscience is like a sentry. It has a post, with strict orders to man that post, and it will not swerve from its duty. Another soldier may come by and say, "Listen, the war's over. Put down your armor and celebrate." But the conscience always remains in place. It answers, "I'm not going anywhere until I hear from the captain. My job is to stay right here and keep a close watch. I will not move unless I get orders from the top."

If we are honest, we all recognize the work of our consciences in our lives. I know that whenever I sin—when I am tempted and I fail—I descend into the depths that David described. I am plagued with guilt and I am filled with nagging fear at the thought of standing before Christ as my judge. I am disturbed and troubled, with no peace or rest in my mind, soul or body.

My conscience is only doing what it has been assigned by God to do. It is condemning me for my iniquity, putting guilt on me for having committed the sin. It is whipping up condemnation in me because I am guilty of disobeying God's Word and breaking His law. All of this is meant to produce in me a knowledge of my need for pardon and restoration.

Even the God-mandated animal sacrifices in the Old Testament could not quiet the conscience. God's people were never delivered from the "conscience of sins" (Hebrews 10:2). Hebrews tells us that in those sacrifices there is a remembrance again made of sins every year (see verse 3). The conscience still had dominion to condemn both the sin and the sinner, and the Israelites' consciences continually cried out, "You are guilty."

Under the New Covenant the blood of Christ did what no other blood sacrifice could do. At the cross, with the very first drop of Jesus' blood, the fountain of God's forgiveness opened. Out of Calvary came the cleansing, sanctifying blood that every follower of Christ has trusted in for two thousand years. At the cross Jesus' blood stripped the conscience of its rights and duties to condemn me as a sinner. So now, because of God's forgiveness, my conscience no longer has that mandate in my life.

Of course, my conscience has retained its right to condemn the sin in me. In fact, that power only increased at Calvary. I now see my sin as increasingly vile and grievous to the Lord and I abhor my sin more than ever. Indeed, I find myself agreeing with my conscience about my sin's deceitfulness and about God's wrath against it. I thank the Lord for giving me a conscience that has not been seared, and I can honestly say I want my conscience to keep exposing my sin and revealing it to me as exceedingly sinful so that I can bring it to the light and repent of it.

Likewise, your conscience has greater authority than ever to reveal to you your sin's exceeding wickedness. The difference is that, while your conscience can remind you of your sin, it can no longer condemn you. You are now under the blood of Jesus Christ. Your conscience can no longer make you tremble. It cannot put any condemnation on you.

The conscience does not want to let go. It will try to keep condemning you, but Christ's blood has all power to quiet it. His cleansing blood tells the conscience, "I'm what you have been waiting for. You are hearing from your captain now, so stop condemning. The war is over on this particular battlefield."

When the devil reminds you of a past sin you may still feel condemned about it. When this happens you have to turn to your conscience and say, "Be quiet. I am under the blood for that sin. I repented of it and it cannot be brought up to me again. Yes, it was ugly and evil. If I ever commit that sin again, I want you to show me just how ugly it is—but you can no longer condemn me for it. God's Word says there is no condemnation toward anyone who is in Christ Jesus and who walks after the

Spirit. I am forgiven by the blood of my Savior. I have trusted in His name—in the God who pardons. I realize that you, my conscience, are constantly aware of sin's power, but I am now free from your power to condemn me."

Forgiveness Without Repentance?

In many churches God's mercy and forgiveness are the only topics ever preached from the pulpit. The pastors state, "God is good. He is all about mercy and He has forgiven us all." These ministers preach God's mercy and forgiveness without ever mentioning repentance or allowing their congregants to repent.

The people in these churches have never experienced a genuine soul-shaking by God's living Word. Nor have they listened to the voice of their consciences. They are not allowed to point out their sins and reveal the severity of God. Thus, the Holy Ghost cannot allow the law to complete its convicting work in them.

Instead the people try to appropriate forgiveness without ever facing their sins. They never see how exceedingly vile and wicked their sins are. As a result, they end up thinking of God as being like themselves. In their eyes, He is like a doddering old grandfather who overlooks the sins of those who merely do their best.

You can see the error of these people's ways revealed in their lives. They have no desire to do battle with their sins. They are never stirred or moved to give up their iniquities, and they have no desire or hunger to become more like Jesus. They are not led to mortify their sins through the power of the Holy Spirit.

These people have appropriated a false peace and, in many cases, they have seared their consciences. They do not want to do any soul-searching. They do not want to be troubled by their sins or deeply convicted over them. All they want is immunity from hell, so they have choked off the convicting work of the Holy Ghost who works in tandem with the conscience. The

Bible states that such people convince themselves, "I have peace, though I walk in the stubbornness of my own heart." Scripture also describes them as "turning the grace of our God into lasciviousness" (Jude 4). Show me a Christian who is not deeply convicted by his sin, and I will show you someone who knows nothing about true biblical forgiveness. You never find this person digging deeply into God's Word. He is never drawn toward the closet of prayer. Instead he is cozy with the world and he does not show any kind of deep desire for Jesus.

Things are much different in churches where true forgiveness through repentance is preached. The result there is greater obedience, more passionate devotion and an ever-increasing love for Christ.

How God's Forgiving Name Was Revealed

All of the blood sacrifices in the Old Testament were meant to teach God's people about the Lord's forgiving nature. Each of these sacrifices had to do with *propitiation* and *atonement*—which both mean "forgiveness."

No animal sacrifice could take away a person's sin and offer total pardon, but these sacrifices did foreshadow a future redemption. Every offering pointed to the Lamb of God who would come as a sacrifice to take away the sins of the world. At God's appointed time His own Son, Jesus, gave His life as an offering. Afterward the people of God stood under Christ as their banner of forgiveness.

Leviticus 16 shows us one of the most solemn of all the sacrifices in Israel: the sin offering. God had instituted this event with the intent to explain to His people something of His nature and character. The entire ceremony was about His readiness and willingness to forgive.

For this occasion God called together all the tribes of Israel to gather before the tabernacle. Then two goats were brought out in front of the assembly. These animals were presented to the Lord at the door of the congregation as an offering for sin. One of the goats was to be sacrificed on the altar and the other was to serve as the scapegoat that would carry away the people's sins.

As the first goat was led to the outer court to be sacrificed, the second goat was held outside by an able-bodied man. After sacrificing the first goat, the high priest approached the second goat and laid his hands on it. Scripture describes the scene this way:

> When he hath made an end of reconciling the holy place, and the tabernacle of the congregation, and the altar, he shall bring the live goat: and Aaron shall lay both his hands upon the head of the live goat, and confess over him all the iniquities of the children of Israel, and all their transgressions in all their sins, putting them upon the head of the goat, and shall send him away by the hand of a fit man into the wilderness: and the goat shall bear upon him all the iniquities unto a land not inhabited: and he shall let go the goat in the wilderness.
>
> Leviticus 16:20–22

Do you get the picture? All of Israel stood watching as the high priest placed his hands on the goat's head and began confessing the people's sins. I imagine the priest saying the following, in so many words: "I lay all the sins of this people on the head of this animal—all disobedience, all adultery, all covetousness. . . ." When the priest finished praying, the strong man who held the goat then led the animal away toward the outside of the camp.

At this point I picture God's people parting on either side, making a way for the goat to come through. They watch solemnly as the animal is led out of their midst. Finally it crosses the boundary of the camp. Then the strong man leads it over a hill and into the distance, far beyond the people's sight. It is being taken into an uninhabited land, to a deep ravine with no way out for the goat. That way the animal will never come back and haunt God's people by causing them to remember their sins. (This illustrates the word that Micah spoke to God's people: "Thou wilt cast all their sins into the depths of the sea" [Micah 7:19].) Can you imagine what happens next? How the people must shout as the goat disappears over the hill: "There go our sins! There go our sins!"

What joy there must have been among God's people on that day! Please understand, the Lord Himself instituted this ceremony. His people were bound by His commandment to observe it. So for the next four thousand years the Lord spoke a clear message through these sacrifices: "I am the God who forgives all sin." He was declaring to the whole world, as well as to His people: "I am forgiveness, and when I forgive you I remove your sins from My sight forever."

As you probably realize, the two goats in this ceremony represent our Lord Jesus. He came both as the perfect sacrifice and as our scapegoat—offering His life in exchange for ours and taking away all our sins. The Bible tells us that God laid on His own Son's head the guilt of all our sins: "The LORD hath laid on him the iniquity of us all" (Isaiah 53:6).

Do you doubt God's forgiveness? If so, you need to have your own solemn assembly. When the enemy comes at you with condemnation and guilt over some past sin, go to your secret closet of prayer. Then place yourself in the awesome scene that took place in Israel.

Imagine yourself standing in the crowd, watching the two goats at the door of God's house. You see one goat being led inside to be sacrificed. Then you see the high priest laying his hands on the head of the other goat. You listen as the priest confesses your sins over the scapegoat.

Picture the able-bodied man leading the goat away. Watch as they cross beyond the borders of the camp and slowly disappear. Then, as they fade from view, shout, "There go my sins! There go my sins!" Let the truth sink in: "My sins are gone forever.

They can never be used against me again, and they can never come back to haunt me. The Lord has removed them from my life forever."

The Lamb of God has taken all of your sins upon Himself and His sacrifice for you is good once and for all:

> Neither by the blood of goats and calves, but by his own blood he entered in once into the holy place, having obtained eternal redemption for us. For if the blood of bulls and of goats, and the ashes of an heifer sprinkling the unclean, sanctifieth to the purifying of the flesh: how much more shall the blood of Christ, who through the eternal Spirit offered himself without spot to God, purge your conscience from dead works to serve the living God?
>
> Hebrews 9:12–14

Proof of This Forgiveness in His Name

Think about it: What kind of God would our Lord be if He commanded a sinful people to humble themselves and repent, but then left them waiting at the altar? If the Lord called us to repent when there was no way out for us—no deliverance from our guilt and shame—He would not be a just, loving God. The very repentance to which He calls us implies forgiveness; indeed, it insists upon it. Wherever there is repentance, forgiveness has to be found. His call for us to repent is proof, therefore, that He forgives. Otherwise, the Gospel would be a lie.

We must believe that God forgives us when we repent. In fact, no repentance is acceptable to Him unless it is accompanied by faith in His forgiveness.

It is amazing that many Christians have confessed their sins without ever receiving an understanding of forgiveness. They have been convicted of their sins, they have confessed them, wept over them and been sorry for committing them. They have asked God to deliver them from their sins, and in some cases they have even made restitution for them. But they have never received a sense of God's pardon for their iniquities.

We see many examples of this in Scripture. I think of Cain, Pharaoh and Ahab, to name just a few—and of course there is Judas. The Bible says that after Judas betrayed Christ, he "repented himself" (Matthew 27:3). This man showed all the signs of heartfelt repentance. He confessed: "I have sinned" (verse 4). He named his sin: "I have betrayed the innocent blood" (verse 4). He even made restitution, returning the thirty pieces of silver he had accepted for betraying the Lord (see verse 3). Why then didn't Judas' repentance bring him peace? Scripture tells us that immediately after Judas did these things, he "went and hanged himself" (verse 5).

What was missing in Judas' repentance? It was this: Judas believed his sin was too grievous to be forgiven. He simply could not believe that a vile sin like his own could ever be pardoned. In short, he did not have true faith in God's forgiveness. Judas' act of suicide stated, "My sin is too wicked, too hopeless ever to be forgiven." He could not accept the thought that he could ever be pardoned for betraying Christ, so he took his own life.

In the same way, multitudes of sinners hang themselves on a tree of hopelessness. They go through the motions of life, but they have already given up hope. They may repent with tears; they may be truly sorry for their sins, naming and confessing every transgression, even making restitution as far as is humanly possible. But if they have not trusted in God's forgiveness, all their acts of repentance are in vain.

You may think that you cannot be forgiven because of the awfulness of your sin. Perhaps you are convinced that your trespasses have been too deep and numerous for God to pardon. Let me remind you that God's call for us to repent is proof that He forgives. He cannot deceive.

You may answer, "But you don't know the depths of the sin I have committed. If you only knew the things I have done in secret. You know nothing about my hardness, my rebellion, my wicked thoughts. You cannot imagine the kind of blasphemy I've committed. My heart is filthy, and I fall back into my sin all the time. There is no use in my even trying to approach God for forgiveness. I'm too far gone."

I say, "Try telling that to the apostle Paul." This man confessed that he had been a blasphemer and the chief of all sinners (see 1 Timothy 1:13, 15). The Bible is filled with further proof that God has forgiven the worst of sinners. Look at these two:

> Know ye not that the unrighteous shall not inherit the kingdom of God? Be not deceived: neither fornicators, nor idolaters, nor adulterers, nor effeminate, nor abusers of themselves with mankind, nor thieves, nor covetous, nor drunkards, nor revilers, nor extortioners, shall inherit the kingdom of God. And such were some of you: but ye are washed, but ye are sanctified, but ye are justified in the name of the Lord Jesus, and by the Spirit of our God.
>
> 1 Corinthians 6:9–11

> Let the wicked forsake his way, and the unrighteous man his thoughts: and let him return unto the LORD, and he will have mercy upon him; and to our God, for he will abundantly pardon.
>
> Isaiah 55:7

These passages also apply to the believer who has fallen back into a grievous sin. Such a person finds himself saying, "I knew better than to do this. I had been so convicted and I had made so many promises to God. Now I've fallen back again and this time it seems to be one time too many. There is no way God could forgive me for sinning against the light as I have. I can't help thinking that I have sinned against the Holy Ghost. I have grieved Him so many times. How could God possibly forgive me now, after I've done this over and over?"

Beloved, go back to God's Word. Forsake your sinful ways. Return to the Lord in repentance and believe that He will pardon you abundantly once again. If you have read the passages above but are still unwilling to believe that your sin can be forgiven, then you are faking your grief. You must simply want an excuse to stay in your sins!

I say to every homosexual, every lesbian, every transvestite, every sadomasochist, every rapist, every child molester—even the worst of sinners: God does not give up on anyone. His Word says that He is not willing for anyone to perish—not one person! He calls you to repentance. He wants you to know Him by His name—*the God who pardons*—because He wants to heal you and set you free.

So don't say, "My sin is too powerful." Don't run from the Lord, and don't you dare do what Judas did. Don't go out and hang yourself on some tree of hopelessness. Jesus Himself says, "Wherefore I say unto you, All manner of sin and blasphemy shall be forgiven unto men" (Matthew 12:31).

There Are No Hopeless Cases

Years ago I almost gave up hope for homosexuals and others who struggle with sexual perversions. Our ministry had started a home for recovering homosexuals, but it ended up becoming a nest of iniquity. Even the director, who was supposedly delivered from his homosexuality, turned back to his old lifestyle. Eventually we had to shut down the home.

I resigned myself to thinking, *This kind of ministry is hopeless.* Over the years, however, I have met more and more individuals who once were bound by homosexuality and now have found freedom in Christ. At one time they thought the only thing they could do was to come out of the closet and give themselves over to their sin. They let the devil convince them that there was no hope for their lives, no victory available to them. But God never gave up on them. He found them in their sinful state and He assured them, "There is hope for you. The blood of Jesus Christ has power to cleanse you."

You may be disheartened by certain Old Testament warnings like "[God] will laugh at your calamity; [He] will mock when your fear cometh" (Proverbs 1:26). You have to understand that these passages are written only to those who mock and refuse God's call to repentance. Some people have turned their backs on His offer of forgiveness and restoration. But if your heart is open to God's voice—even if you once mocked—He will not reject you. The Lord will hear your cry.

Moreover, God's pardon has a supernatural effect. When you come to Him in true repentance, believing He will forgive you, He will fill your heart with a love for Him and a hatred for sin. You will never want to go back to your habit again. At times you may be tempted by it, but God's forgiveness will build strength into you day by day.

Perhaps you have come to a place where you have accepted these terms of forgiveness, but now you are plagued by fear: "I'm afraid that if I ask God to forgive me I'll go straight back to my sin." That fear has been put in you by the enemy. Above all, Satan wants to keep you from receiving the Father's forgiveness. Your role is to go to the Father, regardless. He will give you the strength to deal with each temptation as it comes. You only need to face one day at a time. Jesus told us, "Sufficient unto the day is the evil thereof" (Matthew 6:34).

So deal with your sin. Repent and accept God's forgiveness right now. Say to yourself, "I'm forgiven today, and the Lord who has kept me today is going to keep me tomorrow, too. Day by day, He is going to give me all the strength I need."

Would He Deprive His Own Children?

The Lord has revealed Himself to the ungodly as a God who pardons. Why would He deny that revelation to His own children?

Perhaps you love Jesus, yet you are troubled in heart. You are under a heavy weight of guilt because you have fallen into a particular sin. You may be so cast down that you are not even able to look up. Once again, you have done the very thing you hate, and you have grieved the Holy Spirit. Now there's a breach between you and the Lord. Your sweet communion with Him has become clouded.

You may know other Christians in the same situation. They also trusted in God's forgiveness at one time, when they first came to Christ. But now that they have sinned as believers, they find it hard—even impossible—to believe God will forgive them. Some have lived for years in fear and dread, always afraid that the Lord is mad at them. Since their first year of walking with Jesus, they have never enjoyed the peace, joy and gladness that comes from trusting in His pardon and mercy.

We must realize that God offers us terms of reconciliation that He did not even offer to fallen angels. Those creatures had been holy, pure, obedient worshipers of God, but when they fell into sin they were not offered any way of escape: "God spared not the angels that sinned, but cast them down to hell, and delivered them into chains of darkness, to be reserved unto judgment" (2 Peter 2:4).

To all who know the Lord, He offers more than terms of reconciliation; He seeks to give us full forgiveness and peace. What amazing grace! The same Lord against whom we have sinned—whose commandments we have broken, whose name we have dishonored, whose love we have trampled—comes to us in mercy urging us to be reconciled. He tells us, "I want you back in sweet communion with Me. I want you once again to enjoy peace, gladness and rest in your soul. So here are My terms: Return to Me, and believe in My forgiveness.

"No matter what your sin, no matter how cast down you are or guilt-ridden you feel, you can return to Me in a moment's time. You will enjoy My merciful pardon: full, free forgiveness. Your condition is not hopeless, so you need not wallow in fear or dread for another hour. I'm offering you these simple terms of reconciliation, if you are willing to accept them."

Forgiveness Is on God's Terms

We may know and accept God's terms of reconciliation, but our flesh can still want to make payment for our sins, somehow, to try to pacify God's anger. It cries out, "How should I come before the Lord to be reconciled? Should I bow before Him? Should I offer Him sacrifices of some kind? How can I do penance? Can I pay for my sin with great self-denial? What can I do to make God happy with me?"

We see this attitude in Naaman, a captain in the Syrian army. Naaman had contracted leprosy. When this good man ran out of all medical hope, God told him that he could still be healed. The Lord's only term, His one condition, was this: "Go and wash in Jordan . . . and thou shalt be clean" (2 Kings 5:10).

These were not terms Naaman wanted to hear. Scripture says that he became angry "and went away in a rage" (verse 12). Naaman was saying, "I don't like God's terms. How could this be so simple? I have been deceived somehow. I want my own terms."

But Naaman's servants challenged him, saying, "If God had told you to do some great thing, you would have done it in a heartbeat. You wouldn't hesitate to do something big, something sacrificial, something powerful in your own strength. Now God tells you to do one simple thing to receive your healing, and you refuse?" (see verse 13).

Many Christians are like Naaman. They have set their own terms for healing and cleansing. They do not want to come to the

Knowing God by Name

Lord on His simple, uncomplicated terms. They will not accept that they are merely to repent, return to the Lord and believe Him for forgiveness. Instead, they say, "I've sinned so badly, I can't believe I'm supposed to just come to God and repent."

Like Naaman we are convinced that God needs some great thing from us before we can be cleansed and forgiven. We tell ourselves that we need to offer weeks of mortification, rivers of tears, days of fasting, nonstop witnessing, giving to the poor and reading the Bible all the way through. Or we think, *I need to spend a few months grieving, sorrowing, weeping before I can even seek God's forgiveness and pardon. I've got to cry until God knows I'm sorry. How else will He know I'm grieved over what I have done?*

We think that we can compensate for our failures, but God has set the only acceptable terms and those terms are simple and uncomplicated. His Word tells us, "Thus saith the Lord GOD, the Holy One of Israel; In returning and rest shall ye be saved; in quietness and in confidence shall be your strength" (Isaiah 30:15).

By repenting, we return to God's rest, but first we have to believe in His forgiveness. This verse in Isaiah tells us, "In confidence shall be your strength," meaning, we have to be confident in God's readiness to forgive. We must be able to say confidently, "My God has forgiven me. I am cleansed, healed, set free—all because He has wiped away my sins forever."

Most Christians have heard these truths hundreds of times. So why don't more of us quickly return to the Lord? Why do we not throw ourselves immediately on His mercy, lay hold of the New Covenant and trust in His promise of Holy Ghost power to overcome sin's dominion? It is because we do not truly trust in His name—the God who pardons.

"They that know thy name will put their trust in thee: for thou, LORD, hast not forsaken them that seek thee" (Psalm 9:10). The God who forgives will never forsake you. If you return to Him, He will reveal Himself to you.

Jesus told us that He came "in my Father's name" (John 5:43). We know the Father's name is forgiveness—*the God who pardons*. Run to Jesus now and receive in faith God's mercy and forgiveness. His pardon in your life depends on your belief in His name—*the God who forgives*.

eleven

His Name Is *Intercessor*

The God Who Maintains Our Peace

What does Scripture mean when it says that Jesus makes intercession for us? I believe this subject is so deep, majestic and beyond human understanding that I tremble even to address it. Biblical scholars hold various views on its meaning, but no book or commentary has begun to satisfy my search. In fact, the more I read on the matter, the more confusing it all sounds.

Nevertheless, through prayer and trust in the Holy Spirit's guidance I am beginning to grasp just a little of this incredible subject. Recently I have been praying very simply, "Lord, how does Your intercession in heaven affect my life? Your Word says that You appear before the Father on my behalf. What does this mean in my daily walk with You? I don't need to know what the great scholars have learned. Just show me a simple truth I can grasp and appropriate for my life."

Let us begin with this scriptural definition of Christ our intercessor: "Wherefore he is able also to save them to the uttermost that come unto God by him, seeing he ever liveth to make intercession for them" (Hebrews 7:25).

The English word *intercession* means "to plead on another's behalf." This speaks of a figure who takes your place before others to plead your cause. When you hear such a definition—that is, an intercessor as someone who pleads for you—do you picture Christ continually pleading to God for you, asking for mercy, forgiveness, grace and blessings? In my opinion, this image makes our heavenly Father appear tight-fisted. I simply refuse to believe that grace has to be pried out of our loving God. If we limit ourselves to such a narrow definition of *intercession,* we will never understand the deeper spiritual meaning of what Christ does for us.

The Bible declares that my heavenly Father knows my needs before I can ask Him. Often, He supplies those needs before I even pray. I find it difficult, therefore, to accept that God's own Son has to plead with Him for anything. Besides, Scripture says that the Father has already entrusted His Son with all things: "In him dwelleth all the fullness of the Godhead bodily" (Colossians 2:9).

The popular evangelical view of Christ's intercession is that Jesus returned to heaven to act as High Priest on our behalf. There is no question about this. The Bible states: "Christ is not entered into the holy places made with hands, which are the figures of the true; but into heaven itself, now to appear in the presence of God for us. . . . Christ being come an high priest of good things to come" (Hebrews 9:24, 11).

Knowing God by Name

I believe Jesus intercedes today to preserve His people, keeping us from sin and maintaining us in God's love. He will not allow anything—any fear, any temporary fall, any accusation from Satan—to alienate us from the Father. In short, He prays for us in the same way He prayed for His disciple Peter: "that thy faith fail not" (Luke 22:32).

Some scholars believe Christ's mere presence in heaven is a kind of silent intercession. In other words, Jesus has already paid the price for our sin, shedding His own blood. Thus, His nail-scarred hands and feet are a perpetual testimony of what He has accomplished on our behalf. I have no problem accepting this picture of Christ's intercession. I have always found it hard to believe that every time I sin or face Satan's accusations, Jesus has to appear before the throne to remind God of His sacrifice. This reflects the Old Testament system, when blood offerings had to be made for sin regularly. It also echoes the sacrifice of atonement—the offering made year after year when the high priest carried blood and incense into the holy of holies to atone for the people's sin.

No, Jesus' sacrifice for us was made once and for all:

> Nor yet that he should offer himself often, as the high priest entereth into the holy place every year with blood of others; for then must he often have suffered since the foundation of the world: but now once in the end of the world hath he appeared to put away sin by the sacrifice of himself.
>
> Hebrews 9:25–26

Note the phrase *but now once*. This settles the matter. When Christ's blood was presented in heaven, it ended the need for any further sacrifice. His blood paid the price for all sin, for all time, and our heavenly Father does not have to be constantly reminded of that fact.

Some Puritan scholars hold yet another belief about Jesus' intercession. They claim that it has to do with the way Christ presents our prayers to the Father. They quote this passage:

> There was given unto him much incense, that he should offer it with the prayers of all saints upon the golden altar which was before the throne. And the smoke of the incense, which came with the prayers of the saints, ascended up before God out of the angel's hand.

> Revelation 8:3–4

This suggests that Jesus "perfumes" our prayers or "filters" them to make them acceptable to the Father. In this way He intercedes for us—or mediates our prayers—before God's throne.

I agree that Christ adds His own incense to our prayers, but not in order to make them acceptable. This is where I find a theological problem. Scripture makes it clear that Jesus' sacrifice has already given us full access to the Father. First, His work on the cross reconciled us to God. He opened to us the holy of holies. Now we are one in Christ; we cannot be separated from Him. We are bone of His bone, flesh of His flesh. His presence in heaven has given us the right to go directly to the mercy seat. In this way we have direct access to the heavenly Father. Jesus Himself said, "In that day ye shall ask me nothing. Verily, verily, I say unto you, Whatsoever ye shall ask the Father in my name, he will give it to you" (John 16:23).

Make no mistake: Jesus is our mediator. But He has already done His work of mediation on the cross. Through His shed blood He has reconciled us to God. Now nothing stands between us and the Father's throne. This is one of the glorious victories Christ won for us at the cross.

A Simple Truth

I certainly do not claim to know everything about Christ's intercession for us, but I do believe that whatever our High Priest is doing in His intercession for us, it is a very simple matter. And I believe that intercession has to do directly with the growth of His Body here on earth. He is at work supplying every joint and part with might and strength.

After much prayer, careful study and reliance on the Holy Spirit, I have concluded this about Christ's intercession for us:

Jesus died on the cross to purchase peace with God for me—and He is in heaven now to maintain that peace, for me and in me.

The peace we have with God the Father through Christ distinguishes our faith from all other religions. Hindus worship thousands of gods. Muslims worship Allah. But in both the Hindu and Muslim worlds there is no peace. Why? These gods are powerless to pardon sin. According to their beliefs, people have to work and strive, hoping and praying they will somehow be relieved of their sins.

In every other religion besides Christianity the sin question is left unsettled. In them, sin's dominion has not been broken; therefore, there can be no peace: "There is no peace, saith the LORD, unto the wicked" (Isaiah 48:22). We have a God who provides peace by pardoning sin.

I am the LORD thy God which teacheth thee to profit, which leadeth thee by the way that thou shouldest go. O that thou hadst hearkened to my commandments! Then had thy peace been as a river, and thy righteousness as the waves of the sea.

Isaiah 48:17–18

This is the very reason Jesus came to earth: to bring peace to troubled, fearful humankind. He testified, "These things I have spoken unto you, that in me ye might have peace" (John 16:33). Before He ascended to heaven, He said, "Peace I leave with you, my peace I give unto you: not as the world giveth, give I unto you. Let not your heart be troubled, neither let it be afraid" (John 14:27).

How does Jesus maintain God's peace for me? He does it in three ways:

First, Christ's blood removed the guilt of my sin. In this sense, Paul says, "He is our peace" (Ephesians 2:14). Jesus made peace for me through His blood, and now I no longer have to tremble in fear at the devil's accusations. I know I have a heavenly Father who forgives and pardons my sin. He invites me to come boldly to His throne of grace, to receive His mercy. "We have access by faith into this grace wherein we stand" (Romans 5:2).

Second, Christ maintains my peace and joy in believing: "Now the God of hope fill you with all joy and peace in believing, that ye may abound in hope, through the power of the Holy Ghost" (Romans 15:13). "Therefore being justified by faith, we have peace with God through our Lord Jesus Christ" (Romans 5:1). We have a God who forgives and pardons and, because of this, we can experience the joy and victory of having peace with the Lord.

Third, Jesus causes me to rejoice at the hope of entering glory: "We . . . rejoice in the hope of the glory of God" (Romans 5:2).

> Having made peace through the blood of his cross, by him to reconcile all things unto himself. And you, that were sometime alienated and enemies in your mind by wicked works, yet now hath he reconciled in the body of his flesh through death, to present you holy and unblameable and unreproveable in his sight.
>
> Colossians 1:20–22

Simply put, peace is the absence of fear—and a life without fear is a life full of peace.

God promised us this kind of peace in the oath He made to Abraham. The Lord pledged to send a redeemer to His people to deliver them from all enemy powers. This redeemer would enable us to live holy lives and be without fear. (See Luke 1:69–75.)

Christ spent His years on earth preaching about and offering the peace of God, and He gave God's peace freely to all who received Him. Peter says Christ "multiplies peace" to us: "Grace and peace be multiplied unto you through the knowledge of God, and of Jesus our Lord" (2 Peter 1:2). Today, all who name Jesus as their Lord have received His divine peace—peace with God and peace within.

Moreover, when Jesus ascended to heaven, He did not just bask in the glory that God bestowed on Him. He did not take His place of power at the Father's right hand merely to exult in His triumph. No, He went to the Father to maintain the hard-won peace He achieved for us at Calvary.

Multitudes of Christians do not live by this truth. They live in terror, always upset, worried about their salvation, letting their consciences condemn them. But Scripture says, "He ever liveth to make intercession for them" (Hebrews 7:25).

Our Savior is alive in glory right now, and He is both fully God and fully human, with hands, feet, eyes and hair. He also has the nail scars on His hands and feet and the wound in His side. He has never discarded His humanity; He is still a man in glorified body—and right now our Man in eternity is working to make sure we are never robbed of the peace He gave us when He left. He is ministering as our High Priest, actively involved in keeping His Body on earth full of His peace. When He comes again, He wants us to "be found of him in peace" (2 Peter 3:14).

A Double Threat

Two things threaten my peace with God and both involve sin: my conscience and Satan's accusations. First, my conscience troubles and accuses me, and rightly so. Second, Satan's accusations put fear in me. I believe these are the two primary areas where Christ's intercession applies to us.

My High Priest will not permit my conscience to hold me captive. As we saw in the previous chapter, He interdicts the conscience's condemning power. Nor will He allow Satan's accusations against me to go unchallenged. Christ is my advocate with the Father against every accusation from hell.

What exactly is an advocate? It is simply my friend in court. For Christians, this friend in court is also the Son of the Judge. In addition, our advocate is our brother. In fact, we are set to inherit the Judge's fortune along with Him. Does this mean the Judge is my Father as well? Yes, He is by my adoption.

So this Judge is not adversarial with me at all. The truth is, He loves me as much as He loves His own Son. He is clearly not on the plaintiff's side, but on mine.

Don't misunderstand, however; this is not a rigged court. Although I am related to the Judge, He is absolutely just and holy, without exception. Suppose there is enough evidence stacked against the accused to send him to the electric chair. The Judge cannot just say, "This man seems awfully sorry. I know there's a lot of evidence against him, but I can't help feeling sympathy for him. He cries a lot. Besides, I hate to see his family suffering through this trial. This is really painful to Me. I feel merciful toward him. I've decided that I am going to dismiss all charges."

What judge anywhere would get away with this? Justice would be perverted.

In a recent poll, 82 percent of Americans said they do not believe a person can get justice unless he has a lot of money and a powerful team of lawyers. Apparently, people do not believe in justice anymore. God still does, however, and He would never pervert His divine justice in this way. If He is eternally just, His justice has to be satisfied. Everything decided in His court must be according to divine justice. No human or devil can ever accuse Him of showing favoritism. His justice will be meted out according to His divine law, with every debt paid in full.

It is important for us to realize that there are two courtrooms. The first court is in our hearts, where our consciences accuse us. The second court is in heaven, where Satan accuses us before the

Father. I believe Jesus' intercession takes place in both courts. Jesus, the Man in glory, deals with Satan's accusations and, while the human Christ cannot come down and deal with my conscience, His Spirit in me can. So you see, Jesus' work for us is not confined to either heaven or earth.

Christ's work of intercession for us includes something I have already mentioned: interdiction. This means to prohibit by placing under a legal sanction—or, in lay terms, to halt an action by a court order. It means getting a court order from a judge to stop someone's actions against you.

Here is how I see interdiction working in our lives. When we sin, we break God's law. God's laws are unchangeable. They are the heart of His glory and He has to honor them. The Ten Commandments represent His moral law, and that law demands justice or payment. One of these laws states, "Thou shalt not commit adultery" (Exodus 20:14) and the law adds, "The adulterer and the adulteress shall surely be put to death" (Leviticus 20:10).

You have to understand that we are not subject to the law as a means to salvation. In other words, we could not be saved by keeping the law perfectly. Rather, the law rules over our lives as boundaries of our behavior, and if we cross those boundaries, we commit sin.

The Law Saves Nobody but Convicts Everybody

You cannot fool your conscience. It has been trained by God in the divine law and knows it well. As I stated previously, the conscience abides by God's law without partiality. Like a sheriff of the soul, it has to arrest and charge every lawbreaker.

The conscience is no threat to law-abiding people, but if you break the law, your soul-sheriff springs into action. God has commissioned this sheriff to handcuff you, bring you to prison and not release you until the Judge says that justice has been served. It is nothing personal; the sheriff is just doing his job. He will not be prejudiced. He has to abide by the law.

The job our consciences perform is actually a wonderful work of God. He brings the law to us to show us the awfulness of our sin. Otherwise we would develop a hard heart.

An unrighteous person may try to bribe his conscience. The Bible calls this searing the conscience (see 1 Timothy 4:2). This means rendering your conscience insensitive to the law so that you excuse any violation. In this case, your conscience releases you without charging you. It simply overlooks your sin. People who have seared their consciences "let themselves go" in regard to morality. But if you are a godly person, your soul-sheriff cannot be bought. He will arrest you and show you how exceedingly serious your sin is. Then he will remind you that the law always seeks a penalty of death.

Have you never been imprisoned by your conscience? Have you never felt the agony and pain of sinning against almighty God? Have you never been burdened by shame and sorrow because you have broken God's law and must pay the penalty for it? My soul-sheriff comes after me on many occasions. No matter what my failure may be, he is there shouting, "Guilty, wicked, unholy!" He reminds me that I face God's wrath.

At the same time that my conscience arrests and imprisons me, Satan stands in the heavenlies accusing me: "The accuser of our brethren . . . which accused them before our God day and night" (Revelation 12:10).

You may wonder why God allows the devil to approach His throne with accusations against any of His children. Why doesn't God simply ignore the charges that Satan brings against us? Speaking as a natural father, that is what I would do. I would not tolerate anyone's gossip about my children. I would banish that person from my presence, saying, "I don't have to listen to your lies. Get lost."

If the person who knocks at my door has a police officer with him, however, I will be inclined to listen. You see, if my child's accuser can back up his accusations with legal charges then they are no longer gossip. That officer is standing there for a reason. Now it is a legal matter.

This is how Satan operates. He can only approach the Lord about us in legal terms. If his charges are true—if his accusations are based on actual guilt—then God must give him a hearing. (Satan had to falsify his charges against Jesus, who had no sin, but we are all guilty of sin so the devil does not have to accuse us falsely.)

A number of years ago an abortion clinic in New York City was picketed by a group of pro-life demonstrators. The clinic was located in a high-rise office building that also housed some of our church offices. The building owners disapproved of the clinic and finally succeeded in closing it down due to a huge amount owed in back rent.

In anger, the people who ran the clinic sued our church, blaming us for hurting their business! They presented the judge with a long list of false charges, claiming that I had rallied the pro-life demonstrators and that our church had sponsored them.

Because of this lawsuit, I had to give a deposition (a testimony under oath). I had to listen to all the charges and I was asked to reply, but the case never went to trial. The judge threw it out, finding no evidence of guilt.

Likewise, Satan knows he cannot come to God accusing us with trumped-up charges. He knows our righteous Judge would never listen to spurious allegations. What earthly judge would allow a lawyer to come back to his court time after time, presenting foolish accusations? Justice would be offended, and no judge would waste his time on such charges. So do you think for a moment that God would allow the devil to come into His presence just to prattle gossip against us? The Lord would throw him out on his ear!

Satan cannot accuse you before God's throne unless you are truly guilty. When he has a legal claim, he has a right to bring it to our Father. God is just; He will abide by His divine law. Whenever the devil comes to the Father to accuse you, it is because he has caught you breaking God's law. Before he comes to court, he makes sure that he is informed on all the facts against you. He calls in all his demonic operatives to give him evidence against you.

In Revelation 12:10 the word *accuser* means "plaintiff." This is a legal term for someone who brings up charges in court. Satan brings charges especially against those who are truly righteous in Christ. He makes sure that he goes after the devoted one who has fallen into iniquity, sinning against the light, because he sees this as his best chance to hurt someone who is wholly surrendered to the Lord.

Believe me, when Satan goes to God's court he goes heavily armed with evidence. He carries in a well-documented dossier of facts to back up his charges. His demonic operatives recorded the very hour you sinned, the details of your indulgence, everyone involved and the place where it happened. You know it is all true. You are guilty of every undeniable fact, and your conscience convicts you.

God has allowed Satan to appear in his court for only one reason: He is going to shut the mouths of every demonic and human accuser, and He is going to display His holy justice before the world so that He can never be accused of injustice (see Romans 3:19).

Your Advocate in Action

The devil has brought his charges against you. He has piled up evidence upon evidence against you. And you are sitting in prison, crying and weeping, full of shame and guilt. What do you do now? You call your defense attorney, your advocate, your friend in court—Jesus.

When your advocate comes to you, He does not pat you on the back and say, "It's okay. Everything's going to be all right. Don't worry, I'll take care of it." No, He looks you in the eye and says, "Before I can do anything for you, I have to hear from you: Are you guilty? I know you are guilty and the Judge knows you are guilty, but do you know it? I cannot go to court and present a case against your opponent unless the truth has been acknowledged. So, do you acknowledge your sin and repent?"

You tell your lawyer everything: "Yes, I'm guilty. I did it—I sinned. I don't have any defense; I knew full well that I was breaking the law. I have been living in fear because I know I'm condemned. I realize justice has to be done and I know my penalty is death. Anything less wouldn't be just."

At that point, Jesus begins to intercede in the court of your heart. He must be persuaded that you are sorry—that you are admitting your guilt and repenting. Then Christ's Spirit begins to groan in you, making sounds so deep they cannot be understood. This is the Spirit of Christ praying to the Father: "The Spirit also helpeth our infirmities: for we know not what we should pray for as we ought: but the Spirit itself maketh intercession for us with groanings which cannot be uttered" (Romans 8:26).

I have experienced this kind of groaning in the Spirit. When I was a younger man, my sins always prompted my conscience to bring a heavy burden of shame and conviction upon me. I remember driving along once when suddenly I began weeping. I had to pull off the road. I thought, *Where is this coming from?* There was a groaning in my heart, a cry over sin by the Spirit that manifested in me as literal tears. I wept uncontrollably.

Even when it was over I did not understand it. Eventually I learned that it was Jesus, my intercessor. He was groaning to the Father in a spiritual depth I knew nothing about: "I'm not letting David go. I'll bring him to repentance." This is a picture of Christ's amazing intercession taking place right where I live, in my heart.

Have you experienced this? Has some sin of yours been simply too much to handle? Were you in over your head, thinking that you were going down for good, when Jesus' Spirit came to you and said, "I have to answer all the devil's charges"? If so, He began praying and interceding for you, groaning through you, telling the Father, "Keep this one, Lord. Humble him. Break this power over him." That was your High Priest, standing in His temple, interceding for you.

Now You Stand Trial

God your Judge knows that the charges against you are true. Your lawyer, Jesus, knows they are true, too, and does not bother to plead for you before the Judge. Rather, He must interdict the plaintiff, Satan. It is up to your advocate to prove that your accuser has no case. His intercession in this court has to do with satisfying divine justice and with God's right to offer free pardon for your proven sins.

Jesus has His own evidence in hand. First, He has your repentance, your godly sorrow. Second, He has the indwelling of His own Holy Spirit in you, to keep you from going back to your iniquity.

The devil proceeds. He names the charges, going straight to the law to point out what is written about your sin: "It's right here, God: Adulterers must be put to death. I have every proof against this man. You know full well what happened, God. You're omniscient. You cannot deny that I've got the goods on this person."

Now your lawyer turns to the Judge. The Father merely looks at His Son as if to say, "Tell him what You've got."

Your advocate already knows this is strictly a legal matter so He turns to the plaintiff and agrees with him. "Yes, My client is guilty," He says. "He has broken the law. I know more about it than you do, devil. So, if it's the law you want, Satan, I'll give you the law.

"You must know that the law makes provision for a substitutional atonement. After all, if one Adam could bring down guilt on all of humankind, a second Adam could bring salvation to all who believe.

"This law allowed for everyone's sins to be borne by a sacrificial animal. A goat was taken to the altar where it was sacrificed, its blood shed, its life taken, its body consumed. Meanwhile, another goat—or 'scapegoat'—was sent into the wilderness bearing the people's sins. After that the people's transgressions were gone forever. That was the law.

"But now the blood of a perfect substitute has been provided, and it has washed away the sins of all who trust in God. It is written, 'It pleased the LORD to bruise him; he hath put him to grief . . . [and] made his soul an offering for sin . . . and he bare the sin of many, and made intercession for the transgressors' (Isaiah 53:10, 12). Furthermore, it is written, 'By one offering he hath perfected for ever them that are sanctified' (Hebrews 10:14).

"Yes, God's law is holy and just. The lawbreaker must die for his sin. But, you see, Satan, a substitute has come to stand in for this guilty man before you, and that substitute has already paid the price for the man's sin. One has already paid the death penalty. The full demands of the law have been satisfied. This man is now guiltless. He is absolutely free."

At that point your advocate holds up His hands for the plaintiff to see. He states, "On this proof I rest My case: these nail scars on My hands, the scars on My feet, the wound in My side. I am the sacrifice, devil. You know I have paid all his debts. You have no case against My client."

Talk about an interdiction! Here we see the presence of a crucified Man in glory, with marks on His body. This is the grand and glorious voiceless intercession of Christ, and it ends all charges against you.

No more can be spoken against you now. You can shout, "My case is over—finished! Jesus' blood has blotted out all my transgressions and I'm a free man! The devil has nothing on me!"

Beloved, there is only one way we can regain our peace with God and maintain it. We must deal with the devil's accusations in legal terms. We can scream at Satan all day long, binding him, trampling him, ordering him around, but empty threats and human zeal have no power over him. He accuses us in legal terms, and we have to answer him likewise. We must deal with him in a language he fully understands: He must be bound with truth.

God's Word is the legal truth by which we silence Satan. It is the legal document that declares our innocence and we are to stand on it at all times. After all, Scripture was the legal language Jesus used to befuddle and defeat Satan during His wilderness temptation: "It is written. . . ." God's Word remains the legal authority that sends the devil fleeing.

I know a wonderful Christian couple who were sued by hostile plaintiffs. Their case ended up being thrown out for lack of evidence. But that was only the beginning of the couple's problems. The plaintiffs started a campaign of harassment against them. They obtained legal letterhead and wrote threatening letters, saying, "It's not over. We're reopening the case and filing new charges. We're going to sue you for everything you've got."

At one point, a private detective began following the couple. They were terrified, overwhelmed, unable to sleep. Both husband and wife came close to having nervous breakdowns. Why? They had forgotten about the legal document they were given when the case was thrown out. The judge had handed them their formal release, declaring them innocent of all charges.

They could never be tried again on the same grounds. That was the law.

Case Closed

The same is true for you. Satan has lost his case against you, and you have the Judge's document to prove it: God's Word. Now the devil cannot hurt you where it counts, before the Judge's throne on Judgment Day. But you have to rely on God's Word and trust in it. You must stand up to your accusers and read them your document of release.

Your soul-sheriff, the conscience, abides by the law, and because Christ has proven legally that you are free, you can show the sheriff your release document. When he sees you have been declared free, he will move on to other work.

The devil is another matter. He will rage over his defeat, threatening, "I may have lost the case in court, but I will win the battle in your mind." He will harass and threaten you. He will have agents track you. He will tell you that God is mad at you. He will trump up false charges in your mind and make you feel unworthy. He will flood your mind with doubts, fears, lies from hell: "You're unclean. I don't care what anybody says. You know it in your heart."

That is when you have to go on the offensive. Turn to your legal document. Trust it, stand on it. Never believe the devil's lies against you. Find the law of Christ, chapter and verse, and throw it in Satan's face: "When Jesus won my case, He gave me this legal document, devil. It says: 'It is written. . . .' I cannot be tried for the same charges ever again. So you cannot accuse me with this same sin. The Judge has thrown out those charges for good. It cannot go back to court. I live, therefore, with the full assurance that my sins are forgiven. My sin question is settled forever."

Let no one—no devil, no human, no voice of conscience—rob you of the peace Christ has given you. "Who is he that condemneth? It is Christ that died, yea rather, that is risen again, who is even at the right hand of God, who also maketh intercession for us" (Romans 8:34).

Praise God for Christ's dual intercession—in the court of your heart and in the court of heaven! Jesus has you covered on all fronts.

Hallowed be His names.

The Reverend **David Wilkerson** is perhaps best known for his early days of ministry to young drug addicts and gang members in Manhattan, the Bronx and Brooklyn. His story is told in *The Cross and the Switchblade*, a book he co-authored in 1963 that became a bestseller. The story has been read by more than fifty million people in some thirty languages and 150 countries. In 1969 a motion picture of the same title was released.

David Wilkerson has authored more than thirty books in all, including *Vision, Revival on Broadway, Hungry for More of Jesus, Have You Felt Like Giving Up Lately?* and *The New Covenant Unveiled.*

For more than four decades, the Reverend Wilkerson's evangelistic ministry has included preaching, teaching and writing. A distinctive characteristic of his work has been his direct effort to reach the neediest members of society with help for both body and soul.

Teen Challenge, which he founded in Brooklyn, New York, in 1959, is a biblically based recovery program that, through its 490 centers, has reached youth and adults with life-controlling problems worldwide.

In 1987 the Reverend Wilkerson founded Times Square Church in New York City, where he continues to serve as founding pastor. Now in his seventies, David has been led by the Holy Spirit to exhort pastors and their spouses throughout the nations to renew their passion for Christ. He has conducted ministers' conferences and crusades in Eastern Europe, Italy, Ireland and the United Kingdom.

David Wilkerson and his wife, Gwen, live in New York City. They have four children and ten grandchildren.

For more information about David Wilkerson's ministry or about Times Square Church, contact

World Challenge
P.O. Box 260
Lindale, TX 75771
texas@worldchallenge.org

also by
DAVID WILKERSON

The astonishing
true story of David
Wilkerson's outreach to
New York teens trapped
by drugs and gangs.
Over 14 million copies
in print! Written with
John and Elizabeth
Sherrill.

ISBN 0-8007-9070-7

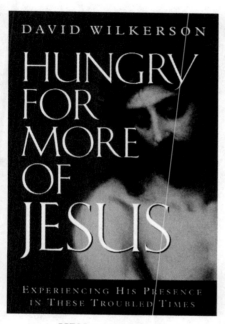

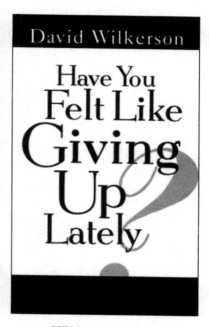

ISBN 0-8007-9200-9

ISBN 0-8007-8481-2

Hungry for More of Jesus, David
Wilkerson's passionate call to a deeper
walk of daily discipleship, invites both
committed and casual Christians to
know Jesus as they've never known
him before.

When grief and depression seem
overwhelming, the founder of Teen
Challenge and World Challenge rec-
ommends a powerful healing process
that restores faith and gives lasting
peace from God.